Improve the Value of Your Home Up to $100,000

Improve the Value of Your Home Up to $100,000

50 Surefire Techniques and Strategies

ROBERT IRWIN

John Wiley & Sons, Inc.

Published by John Wiley & Sons, Inc., Hoboken, New Jersey.
Published simultaneously in Canada.

For general information on our other products and services please contact our Customer Care Department within the U.S. at (800) 762-2974, outside the United States at (317) 572-3993 or fax (317) 572-4002.

Wiley also publishes its books in a variety of electronic formats. Some content that appears in print may not be available in electronic books. For more information about Wiley products, visit our web site at www.wiley.com.

Library of Congress Cataloging-in-Publication Data

Irwin, Robert, 1941–
    Improve the value of your home up to $100,000: 50 sure fire techniques and strategies / Robert Irwin.
        p. cm.
    Includes index.
    ISBN 0-471-22669-6 (pbk. : alk. paper)
    1. House selling.   2. Dwellings—Maintenance and repair.   I. Title.
HD1379 .I6537 2003
643′.7—dc21

                                                              2002032385

Printed in the United States of America.

10 9 8 7 6 5 4 3 2 1

Contents

Dollar signs are used to indicate the likelihood of a technique improving the value of your home: $ = Least boost; $$$$$ = Most likely.

Simple Techniques That Bring Higher Prices and Quicker Sales ... 1

Techniques That Will Improve Neighborhood Values ... 45

Techniques for Making a Grand Entrance   94

Techniques Done with Loving Care   120

Vital Makeover Techniques   145

Techniques That Work in the Backyard   196

Preface

Everyone wants to make money on their home, whether they plan on selling tomorrow or in 5 or even 10 years. Most of us usually consider a home our biggest single investment, and improving its value is high on our list of priorities.

How do you boost your home's value? What can you do to your house that will net you a higher selling price tomorrow . . . or 10 years from now? Should you paint the bedroom? What about putting a gazebo in the backyard? Should you add closet space? Is it possible to do anything about your neighborhood?

Improve the Value of Your Home Up to $100,000 shows you what you can do and how to do it. This book lists 50 techniques that can boost your home's value . . . and they don't necessarily involve spending large amounts of money. Forming a neighborhood action committee (NAC) to improve your entire neighborhood can increase property values by tens of thousands of dollars, yet cost you virtually nothing. Converting an attic or garage to living space can add thousands more, yet cost relatively little. Simply removing a few couches from your living room to make it appear more spacious can increase the home's value hundreds of dollars in the eyes of buyers.

Most real estate books stress buying, selling, or even renovating. This book looks at things differently. It's written from the seller's perspective and emphasizes making money through simple techniques that advance your present home's value.

Of course, your actual result will depend on how well you perform these techniques, what buyers are looking for when you sell, and how hot the market is. However, if you want to sell tomorrow, here are specific techniques you can do today that will immediately convince a buyer your home is worth more. If you want to sell in five years, here's what you can do to keep your home's value up over time.

Don't make the mistake of thinking your home will sell itself for top dollar. It's what you put into it, that will determine how much more you get out.

Simple Techniques That Bring Higher Prices and Quicker Sales

TECHNIQUE **1**   **$$**

Make a better first impression.

Everyone knows that you don't get a second chance to make a good first impression. That's particularly true when it comes to your home.

When you want to sell your property, first impressions are critical. Among real estate people, it is called *curb appeal*. This means that the home looks good when a potential buyer first drives up and parks at the curb. The good impression should continue as they walk through the home.

Real estate agents know that a buy or don't buy decision is often made with that first impression, even though buyers may not realize it until later. If the initial impression of your home is favorable, potential buyers walk through your home thinking positive thoughts. They will be looking for reasons to reinforce their positive feelings—reasons to purchase your home. It will take something really negative to knock them off this first track.

If, however, the first impression is negative, the buyer goes through your house with a mind-set that says, "Show me why I should change that first impression and buy this place." Now the buyer has to be turned around—a much, much harder job.

If you're planning to sell your home, it is imperative that you immediately begin improving the curb appeal of your house. You don't have any time to spare.

If, however, selling your home is just a thought you have for the future, you should remember that creating strong curb appeal doesn't happen overnight. If you start now and work on creating curb appeal over a period of years, the cost will be greatly reduced to say nothing of the stress.

Where to Begin?

Here's a technique that costs you almost nothing, but which will not only give you a quicker sale, it can add extra money to the selling price.

Put yourself in the home buyer's shoes. What do you want to see when you first look at a house?

Beyond a neat, clean appearance, most buyers want to see how their own furniture and things will fit in. It is not uncommon, for example, for buyers to measure the living room to see if their couch will fit in nicely. They may measure the bedroom to see if their furniture will adapt to the room.

If your house is filled with your own clutter, buyers won't be able to visualize putting their things in your home. Your things will be in the way.

Remember, buyers have no imagination. You can *tell* a buyer that her dining room table will fit in your dining room, but if your oversized dining room table is crowding the room with barely space for chairs around it, she's not very likely to believe you.

You want some furniture in each room, otherwise the rooms tend to look small. Furniture makes rooms look not only livable, but gives them proportion.

However, too much furniture and too much clutter makes the room look small. In addition, it makes it look proprietary—it's your room, not theirs. It will be hard for them to visualize it as theirs. You want buyers to see each room as their room. When they do, they'll be more inclined to make an offer on your house. The more they see themselves fitting in, the more they'll want your house and the better that offer will be.

You Don't Have This Problem

You say this doesn't apply to you? Okay, here's a test. Take a minute to look around your home—your living and dining rooms, your kitchen and bath, your bedrooms. Notice anything unusual?

If you answered, "No," then you're like everyone else. We become accustomed to where we live and think of it as perfectly comfortable. If we're comfortable, why shouldn't anyone else be comfortable? If you've lived in a home for a number of years, it is unlikely that you'll see your own clutter.

Now call in a neighbor, friend, relative, or best of all, real estate agent. Ask them to be painfully honest. Ask them not to be polite, not to worry about hurting your feelings. Ask them to look at each room and describe what they see.

At first you might get comments such as,

"That couch is a little big for the room."
"You sure have a lot of knick knacks."
"Why do you have books and things hanging off the shelves of that bookcase?"

"It might be easier to walk through this room if there were fewer tables."

This is what people say when they are trying to be polite—the comments are far worse when they really don't care about your feelings! (Remember, buyers don't care about your feelings.)

My advice is for you to go through every room of your house and take out a third to half of all the furniture.

I can sense the feelings of disbelief coming right through these pages! "A third to a half of the furniture—is he nuts?! There won't be any furniture left."

Trust me, there will be plenty of furniture left. Most people have too much clutter in their homes. Removing a third to a half of it may not be enough! When you've removed a sufficient amount of furniture, boxes, bookshelves, and so on, you'll know it. Your rooms will look barren, empty, as though they are crying out for more things in them.

That's just the way you want it. You want your buyers to sense the need for more so that they can imagine filling those rooms with their furniture. If you can accomplish that, you're well on your way to getting a better offer.

What to Remove

Here is a checklist of the kinds of things you should remove:

Living or Family Room

- *Couches and chairs:* Unless your living/family room is unusually large, one couch and one stuffed chair are usually sufficient.
- *Throw rugs:* If you've got wall-to-wall flooring or nice wood floors, show them off. If you need to cover them, get one large area rug.

- *End tables:* You only need two end tables—one at each end of your couch or chair.
- *Bookshelves:* One bookshelf is usually sufficient. More than that may help hold all your reading, but will not impress most buyers.
- *Ottomans:* They're great for putting your feet on, but otherwise they just take up room.
- *Boxes, bins, cabinets:* These tend to crop up with people who work at home. Get rid of *all* of them. You'll have a new workspace in your next home.
- *Lamps:* One per table and one standing lamp are plenty, unless your room is dark. If it is, then by all means put in more high-powered lamps. This is one case where more light overrules clutter. (See Technique 28.)

Kitchen

- *Countertop:* Clear it off. Keep a few appliances such as a toaster or microwave and get rid of everything else. Particularly get rid of stacks of newspapers, bills, notes, and so on.
- *Doors of refrigerator and cabinets:* Get rid of all those postcards, pictures, and notes that you've got stuck there. Put them inside a drawer, instead of outside it.

Bedrooms

- *Bed and nightstand:* If they are too big for the bedroom, consider moving them out and putting in smaller furniture. (That's what builders of new homes do in many of their model homes.)
- *Table and chair:* Have a table and chair only if the room is large. If not, get rid of it. The same is true for the television and stand.

- *Bureau or dresser:* Be sure there is room for this; if not, get rid of it.

Bathrooms

- *Countertops:* Clean them off. There should be nothing there except, perhaps, a soap dish. No razors, hair blower, deodorant. Store them in shelves and drawers.
- *Floor:* One mat only.
- *Towels:* Bath towels on one rack, smaller wash cloths or face towels on another.

Where Do I Put It All?

If you're like me, we're talking about a lot of clutter. Moving it out is easy. Storing it is hard. One thing you don't want to do is fill up the garage. Buyers like to see plenty of open space in the garage. It tells them your house has adequate storage area as well as room to park car(s).

Other alternatives include storing your extra furniture at neighbors', friends', or relatives'. Rent a storage facility. Give those extra items away. Throw them away. This is a great opportunity to get rid of stuff you really don't need. Think of it as spring cleaning for the whole house.

What If You Have Expensive Furnishings?

The same rules apply, unless you're selling the furnishings with the house. If they're going with you, they can only detract from the house. You might find a buyer who's willing to make you an offer on that Chippendale, but not on the home. Do not distract your buyer; it is the house that is for sale.

TECHNIQUE **2**   **$**

Cars have their place, but not in front.

This is tricky, because there is so much opposition to it. Do not park your car (or have your neighbors park their cars) in the driveway or even in front of the house. Rather park cars in the garage.

"What?" I can hear many readers asking. "That's outrageous. I can park my car anywhere I want. That's my right. It's even written into the Constitution, or should be!"

Let's take it to an extreme and look at it from the buyer's viewpoint. Suppose you're a buyer looking at a house, and an agent takes you into a nice neighborhood. As you drive down the street, there are cars, all makes, models, and ages, parked all over the place. Some are in front of the homes on the street, others are in driveways, and still others are parked on the lawns.

There are guys under some of the cars changing the oil or fixing the transmission. One gal has an engine lift and is hauling the engine out of an old Ford truck, apparently planning to rebuild it. In another case, a group of people are using electric sanders on the body of an old Chevy sanding the paint off, apparently in preparation for doing body work and then repainting.

In short, the neighborhood looks like a repair yard or, at best, a haven for mechanics.

Now remember, you're a home buyer looking for a nice place to live. Would you want to move into that neighborhood? Or would all those cars give you second thoughts?

It's the Sizzle, Not the Steak

Perception can be more important than reality. In our example, the perception is that people don't really care about the neighborhood or in keeping it looking neat and well groomed. Rather, out of financial necessity or simply love of working on their cars, they've turned it into a giant garage. Cars out in front do drive many potential buyers away and can lower property values.

Of course, you say, we're taken an unlikely case . . . or have we? I've driven through neighborhoods that are exactly as described here. Would you buy there? How will you sell there?

While this extreme example helps to make the point, even more moderate examples are telling. When a potential buyer drives into a neighborhood and there's even one car parked on a lawn with someone working on it, it sets a tone. The buyer thinks, "If one could do it, they all could. Do I want to buy into an area where people work on their cars on the front lawn?"

Take it a step further—someone's working on his car, not on the lawn, but in the driveway. He's changing the oil (which almost inevitably means an oil stain). The buyer again asks, "Do I want to buy there?"

Take it yet another step away. Cars are parked in the driveways and in front of the homes up and down the street, but no one's working on them. There are just a lot of cars. If nothing else, the buyer is going to get the impression of a very dense population in this neighborhood. It looks crowded, congested, not the free and open space the buyer might envision as home.

Finally, consider a neighborhood where there are no (or only one or two) cars in driveways and few cars parked on the streets. What does a potential buyer now see? He or she sees the HOMES! They are what stand out. The area looks open, with lots of space (low density). It looks well cared for by owners who are concerned about their neighborhood. In short, it looks like a great place to live. The property values here are likely to be the highest.

I haven't convinced you? Then take a little time to drive around neighborhoods and see for yourself. I would bet that those areas that are most exclusive, that are seeing the fastest price appreciation, that are the most desirable, are also those areas that have the fewest numbers of cars parked in driveways (and, generally, have the fewest number of cars on the street). It's a fact: The fewer autos visible in a neighborhood, generally speaking, the more desirable the area.

Note: We're not talking here about prohibiting people from parking on the street. People have gatherings and parties and those who attend come in cars. But, that's short term and is readily identifiable. Rather, we're concerned about areas where there are loads of cars parked day and night in front and on driveways.

If you need any final convincing, just ask any real estate agent. When your home is listed, you'll be told, "Don't park your car in the driveway or in front. Park it in the garage, so people can see how nice and open your home is."

What to Do?

Obviously, don't park your car in your driveway, or in front on the street for long periods of time. If you don't have a big enough garage for all of your vehicles, you may want to consider renting a covered parking space.

Many homeowners' associations have rules about parking cars. You are requested to keep cars off the driveway and the street and in the garage. Some even go so far as to have a time limit you can keep your car in front of your home.

Although many homeowners complain about such seemingly trivial rules, they also love it when they can sell their homes for higher prices because of the appealing look of their community.

Can you get your neighbors to park their cars in their garages? If you don't have a homeowners' association, this is not the sort of thing you can readily organize a community to do. Most people will simply scoff at the idea.

But, you can help educate your neighbors. Whenever you're with them and conversation inevitably turns to property values, you can be sure people will listen if you have a suggestion as to how property values can be improved. The first time you mention neighborhood appearance and cars, chances are there will be a lot of negative reaction. But, you'll have initiated the idea. When your neighbors travel to other areas, they will now be looking at the interaction of cars and neighborhood appearance. Mention it a couple more times and you'll soon have some converts.

No, you won't be able to turn every neighbor or every neighborhood around. Some areas are simply high density with small garages and too many cars with nowhere to park except the driveway and in front. If that's the case, you'll just have to bear it and the consequences it has on property values.

On the other hand, if you've got your home for sale, keep your driveway clear (and also the front of your home, if possible).

Work on educating your neighbors. If even a few begin to keep their cars parked in their garages, it can make a big change in the overall appearance of the neighborhood.

TECHNIQUE **3**   **$$**

Give your house a friendly look.

This goes right along with curb appeal. No, you can't paint a big happy face on the front of your home without making it seem ridiculous. But, you can make your home more approachable.

Some houses have a warm, wholesome appearance, while others look threatening or at the least unwelcoming. When buyers first see your house, they should get a pleasing impression. It will lead to them into a buying frame of mind, one in which they will pay more money. On the other hand, if they think your place looks like the Addams family's haunted house, they are more likely to shy away, or be willing to consider it only at a bargain price.

What can give a house an unwelcome appearance? There are at least three factors:

1. *Dark colors:* Light colors are in, darker colors are out. If your home is painted a dark brown, dark gray, or something similar, it will not only tend to look old fashioned, but it may also give a sinister impression, one that will cause buyers to shy away. Paint the front of your home a light color. (We'll have more to say on painting exteriors in Technique 14.)

2. *Heavy shrubbery and trees in the front:* These are useful in creating privacy. However, they also can look creepy, even menacing. They can give the house an unkempt look. If you're going to be selling a mansion and you've got a hundred yards between the house and the street, by all means go in for heavy foliage. However, if your house

is more like mine, only a few yards off the street, cut down the shrubs. Let the light shine through, let buyers see your home as they drive up, don't shroud it in secrecy. If you leave things overgrown, at the very least potential buyers will think you need a new gardener, at worst they'll think all the foliage is covering up a problem of some sort.

3. *A difficult approach:* A direct walkway from the street to the front door says welcome, come on in. A circuitous approach that takes you behind trees and along the border of the property tends to say beware! Which impression do you want a buyer to get?

What to Do?

The first thing to do is to cut and trim. This is especially the case if you have bushes and/or trees on the property line in front or on the sides. Some trees can be worse than others.

I once had a friend, Charles, who was buying a house that had tall cypress trees along each front side. They were elegant and stately. However, they also were reminiscent of a cemetery. While this was not particularly a problem near the back of the house, the line of trees strode right out to the sidewalk in front. They were like tall ungainly markers or worse, tombstones, guarding the house . . . from buyers!

When he bought, Charley negotiated a much lower price for the house arguing that it was simply not worth as much as the seller wanted because it looked so bad. The seller, who hadn't had any other offers, had to agree.

As soon as Charley bought the home, he cut down all the cypress trees. It immediately opened up the front. A neighbor even came over and thanked him. She said she had hated them since the previous owner planted them! The cost for cutting them all down was several thousand dollars, but judging by how much influence they had on the price he paid, and the higher price he now could get if he decided to sell the house, it was well worth the money.

Watch Out for Junipers

In the past, it was quite common to plant juniper bushes in front of homes. Owners liked them because they required little maintenance. However, they tended to form a bramble isolating the house from the street.

However, junipers, like dark-colored paints, can date a home. They can also make the house look less inviting. If you have these or similar bushes growing in the front of your house, particularly right up to the street, consider removing them.

You may love your tall trees and dark bushes, but the real question is, Will a buyer?

———————

Note: This does not mean you should not have bushes or trees in front of the house. Colorful plants can add warmth to a home, if placed properly. However, the selection of what to put in front and where to put it is critical. My suggestion is that you hire a good landscaper. Chances are that the hundred dollars or so that a consultation will cost will be well worth the creative suggestions for trimming and replanting, and the resulting better price when you sell. But remember, it takes time to grow new trees and bushes. If you start today, it could still be several years before the plants are large enough to really show off the front of your property.

———————

Your Home's Approach

The approach to your home is yet another matter. If you have a walkway that simply comes off the driveway or if you have a long approach from the side of the property, consider redoing the approach. It doesn't have to cost a large amount. You can make an attractive approach simply by placing large paving stones and allowing grass to grow around them. Be sure to keep the grass trimmed! Old railroad ties look nice in a rustic setting and they tend to be inexpensive. Or, you can go the full route and have a new cement walkway poured.

Whatever course you select, be sure that you spend enough time on the design that the results will enhance the approach to your house and not actually detract from it. Get a landscaper's opinion. Talk to a landscape architect. Go to local building stores and look at the displays. A few hours time spent designing the walkway can make a great deal of difference.

Finally, look carefully at the entrance to the house itself. Do you have a ragged looking covered porch? Are the steps old, cracked wood? Does the banister sag? Is the door cracked or does it need a fresh coat of paint? Is the door handle tarnished?

There are thousands of different ways to create an attractive front entrance to a home. They either enhance the property or make it look worse. Take a look at your entrance with a critical eye. Have a real estate agent give you an opinion—they see hundreds of homes and can often quickly spot a design problem.

You may only need to replace a few boards or apply a new coat of paint. Alternately you may want to install new tile work, add brick trim, or remove a façade that is hiding the true look of your home. (See Technique 23 for a front makeover.)

Stand back and see what, if anything, may be giving your home a sinister, unfriendly look. Then change it for the better. No, you can't really put a big smile on the front of your house. But, if your home front looks good enough, prospective buyers will think it is smiling at them.

TECHNIQUE **4**   **$$**

Fix that lawn.

Potential buyers see the front lawn first—often before they see the house. It's what takes up the most space in front of the typical home. Therefore, your lawn should look terrific. Does your lawn look that good? Does it really?

Most lawns, unfortunately, are sorry things. We just don't have the time to spend working them into really fine shape. You say you have a gardener? Unfortunately, that doesn't guarantee a lush, beautiful lawn. (*Note:* It's not necessary to have a lawn—a rock or cactus garden will do, as long as it fits the character of your neighborhood.)

Get a good landscaper to give you an honest appraisal of your lawn. While you might not mind a lawn that's mostly green with a few yellow patches, to get a sale you want a really lush full lawn that makes a potential buyer want to roll around in it!

The usual problem with a lawn is not enough water. Perhaps you need an automatic watering system. Perhaps reseeding, aeration, and fertilization will do the trick. Find out, and do what it takes.

Replacing a Lawn

If nothing else works, you may need to replace your lawn. There are just two ways to replace a lawn—sod or seed. Sod costs a hundred times more than seed, but you're almost guaranteed an instant, great lawn. Seed can also look terrific, but only if you go through the required preparation of the soil, the watering, fertilizing, and so forth. In either case, you'll need to remove any old grass first. The cost of a new average-sized sod lawn can run $1,500 or more. The cost of seed is only about $50.

Water Is What Counts

Whether you put in a lawn from sod or from seed, it will only grow well if it is watered on a regular basis and watered deeply. Skimp on watering and you might as well forget about improving the value of your home through a new lawn.

If you're retired (or work at home) and can afford to spend an hour or so a day watering your lawn with a hose, then you'll be fine. If you're like most of us, however, you simply don't have the time. Therefore, to get a good lawn, you must first install an automatic watering system.

If you don't have one, I strongly suggest putting in an underground sprinkler system. Obviously, this should be installed *before* you put in your new lawn.

An Automatic Sprinkler System

You may simply want to call in a landscaper and have him install the watering system and the lawn. It's certainly the easiest, though the most expensive way to go. Count on spending several thousand dollars for a good system. You can do it yourself if you don't mind the hard work involved in digging trenches. The major part is easy—almost anyone can glue together PVC pipe.

You can get plans for installing your own automatic sprinkler system at the store where you buy your sprinkler supplies or there are many books available on the subject. Just keep in mind, however, that you need to water everywhere on your lawn. Don't skimp on a system by putting in fewer sprinkler heads only to end up with unwatered brown spots.

Note: Most communities require a building permit when putting in a lawn sprinkler system. The building inspector wants to be sure you use antisiphon valves in your system to avoid polluting your home's potable water system. You will want to be sure to follow health and safety procedures, so proceed with care.

One final word of advice: Be sure to install an automatic device to control your sprinklers, the kind you can set and forget. You can program in which days to water, which stations to water, how long to water each station, and when to skip days. Once programmed, these automatic devices just continue watering away on their own. The cost for the full system is usually not more than a couple of hundred dollars. It is worth it.

The quickest way to improve your curb appeal is to transform a withered, dying, and yellowed lawn into green, lush, and healthy grass. Put in a watering system (if you don't already have one), put in sod or plant seeds and watch your home's value grow.

Note: Some people are absolutely obsessive about weeds in their lawn. They will spend weekends poisoning and digging out weeds and then replanting grass. I wouldn't be that concerned. First impressions do count, as we've said, but they also tend to be superficial. A person driving up to your home may well note whether the lawn is patchy and brown, or solid green and well-mowed. But that person is unlikely to get down and check whether there are weeds in that green sea of grass. You need a good lawn. You don't need a perfect one.

TECHNIQUE **5**   **$**

Add new outside lighting.

It's a mistake to think buyers only come to see your house during the day. As much as 35 percent of the time, buyers view your home at night. In fact, if your house looks particularly attractive at night, you may just have a very powerful selling point. That's a big reason to work on lighting effects.

In Technique 8, we'll talk about putting up a new light fixture in the front of your home as part of enhancing its "jewelry." Here we're concerned with the outdoor lighting itself.

Subdued lighting of the front of a home can make it sparkle after dusk. It can enhance the beauty of the home and make it a showcase. All of this contributes to the visual experience that a potential buyer sees. The value is enhanced with attractive lighting.

Simple Lighting

The quickest and easiest way to get new outdoor lighting is to add Malibu-style lights. These low-voltage lights are manufactured by several companies under a variety of names. They are often on stakes that can easily be driven into the ground. An innocuous black wire trails on the ground (or can be buried just beneath the surface) and connects the lights providing power. The fixture is connected to a house power source and usually has a timer. You can set the lights to go on and off at any time. Many timers allow you several on and off times, as well as the ability to set days and weeks, and they all have a manual override.

Low-voltage lights accent bushes, trees, flowers, and interesting parts of the house front. They give off a small amount of light, just enough to create interesting effects. They also come in a wide variety of colors. With them, you can turn a dull, dark front into an exciting entrance.

Note: Beware of overdoing it with any lights. You don't want your home to look like a grocery store, shopping center, or carnival, all lit up to attract business. Rather, the goal is to provide illumination so your home isn't dark or forbidding looking, and to highlight landscaping and architectural features.

The beauty of Malibu lighting is that because it is low voltage, you don't need an electrician, not usually a building permit, nor any particular skill in connecting it. It's just a matter of sticking the lights into the ground, hooking up the control, turning them on, then focusing them.

However, since you are working with electric current, it goes without saying that you should *be sure the power is off while doing the job.* If you are not qualified to do it yourself, you should get professional help.

Another type of lighting that can work year round are strings of white lights used at Christmas time. Lights that cascade down or even single strands if stretched tactfully, can present a pleasant appearance in any season. You have probably seen trees with these tiny glittering lights all year long at restaurants or in parks, or even on the streets in some large cities.

However, use this type of lighting sparingly. Too much and potential buyers will think you just forgot to take down all of your Christmas lights.

Elaborate Lighting

Beyond low-voltage systems, there are house-voltage lighting systems. Because they produce bright light, these are particularly effective in illuminating driveways and walkways. While overhead lighting can be done, it is usually considered too obtrusive. What is usually more effective are lights that hug the ground. They can show the way and at the same time signal elegance.

The varieties and cost of house-voltage systems are myriad. You can buy fixtures that cost $10 each or ones that cost $200 each. It all depends on how much you want to spend and what effect you want to achieve.

The biggest expense with house-voltage outdoor lighting is putting in the wiring. This normally requires that a deep trench (12 to 18 inches below ground level) be dug and the wires themselves be encased in gray PVC-type plastic or metal conduit.

All connections need to be up to the same building code as for wiring inside your house. Because much of it is underground, there are special wiring considerations. Waterproof junction boxes and connectors are a must.

House-voltage wiring should be handled by professionals. You often need both a landscaper and an electrician to put it in. You will also need a building permit. Again, it should go without saying that you want to be sure the power is *off* when doing any kind of electrical work.

Security Lighting

With increased concerns over crime even in good neighborhoods, many owners are turning to security lighting. Unfortunately, this is often a case where doing more actually results in accomplishing less.

You want to accomplish two goals with security lights. First, you want to light up the front of your home so anyone considering a crime will be discouraged from doing it in front of your place. Second, you want the security lighting to be unobtrusive. You don't want your home to look like a maximum-security prison. Too much security lighting and would-be buyers are going to wonder about crime in your neighborhood, and perhaps be scared away.

What many people do is to buy a halogen high-illumination security light and mount it at the highest point in front of the house, often in front of the garage. It's often on a motion sensor and anyone who comes within a particular radius is immediately drowned in brilliant light. Unless you are living in a high crime area, this may be too much.

It is much better to have a variety of lights and fixtures, all connected to motion sensors. They will go on the moment anyone moves in the front of the house. But, rather than drown the person in light, he or she is simply illuminated in a very easy to see way. The same purpose is accomplished, without transforming your house into a prison-style setting.

At my home, I installed two fixtures on either side of my garage, each containing a 60-watt bulb. The sensor turns them on at dusk and off at dawn. In their dormant state, they give off just enough light to give a subdued illumination to the house. However, when someone walks by and triggers the motion sensor, they immediately go to full brightness, easily illuminating the area. (Motion sensors can be found at almost any hardware store and sell for around $20.)

Combine security with elegance and you've found a quality that adds value to your home.

TECHNIQUE **6** $

Clear out the debris.

How long have you lived in your home? Has it been more than six months? If so, chances are you have already started accumulating debris.

"What debris?" you may be asking.

Simple, it's the old items, junk, leaves, fallen branches, untrimmed and dead flowers and bushes, old wood, forgotten baby carriages, and so on sitting along the sides and back of your home. (If you've got this sort of stuff in front of your home, you've got a real problem!)

It happens gradually, insidiously. In my current home, when we moved in we removed some unsightly beams from the living room ceiling. These were 22-foot-long, 2 by 8 inch pieces of unfinished wood, the sort of thing you'd pay $50 each for if you were to buy them at a building supply store. The people who removed these six beams offered to cut them up so I could use them for firewood. But no, I wasn't about to throw away $300 worth of valuable lumber. So I had them stack the beams along the side of my house. And there they are today, four years later.

Now, if I want to sell my house, what am I going to tell the prospective buyers? "Look, I'm throwing in $300 worth of valuable beams!"

Buyers are not going to see these beams as an asset. They are a liability. If the sight of the beams doesn't help turn them off about the house, they'll certainly begin calculating how much it's going to cost to haul them away. Chances are they'll knock that off the price and insist that I remove them as part of the purchase agreement.

In other words, those beams lower the price. Removing them increases the price. It's just that simple.

Common Debris

Many of us don't actually realize what we have along the side or in back of the house that a buyer might consider to be debris. Here's a list of some of the items that you will want to clear out:

1. Bottles and cans of any sort.
2. Paint cans (whether full of paint or not).
3. Tools (yes, you may need them, but they should be put away, out of sight).
4. Wood, new or used (it doesn't matter that it's for an important project. Just get rid of it so buyers don't see it).
5. Firewood. A small stack looks good since it reminds buyers you have a fireplace. A big stack suggests your other heating system may not be working very well.
6. Cut limbs and branches. Good intentions aside, it's time to get rid of them even if you have to call someone to do it for you.
7. Old appliances. This really looks bad. Face it, you'll never be able to use that old stove or heater, so dump it.
8. Piles of leaves and cuttings. Forget about that compost heap you were intending to start. This just looks like a mess.
9. Rocks, bricks, stones. If you intended to use them for borders or paths, use them now, or else get rid of them.
10. Old planter boxes and pots. Either fill them with flowers and put them in attractive locations, or get rid of them.

11. Old carpeting. Whenever we get new carpeting, it seems like there are always a few pieces of the old carpet (or scraps of the new) that are saved for future(?) use. No buyer wants to see them. Make them disappear.

12. Baby carriages, bikes, carts, skates, skis. Yes, you might need them again and if you're serious about it, have them stored somewhere. If they're not worth the cost of storage, dump them.

13. Newspapers, magazines, books. Do you really ever plan to read them again? Piled in boxes they look terrible and are a source of mildew. Move them out.

14. Old lighting fixtures. Put a new one in, but you can't bear to throw out the old one? Force yourself.

15. Abandoned cars. This is the absolute worst. Sell them or have them hauled away. No buyer wants to think of their future home as a junkyard.

Debris Blocking Drainage

There's a special category of debris that's worth noting that has to do with seemingly innocuous material stacked along the sides of your home. I'm talking of small mounds of dirt, compressed leaves and twigs, or almost anything else.

These sorts of things frequently get forgotten along the sides of the house, particularly when there's no walkway there. They can sit there for years until they get covered with ivy or other ground cover and are forgotten. However, they can have a very detrimental effect on your home.

With almost all houses, water runoff from rain drains from back to front. That means that the water that falls in the back of your yard as well as that which comes off your roof (and is gathered in gutters and goes out down spouts) drains to the street. Usually that's the *only* way it can drain.

However, if you have piles of debris on the side of your home, this natural escape route becomes blocked. As a result, during the rainy season, water can back up along the sides of your home and even in the rear. It can go under your foundation and puddle under your home or in the basement. This can cause your foundation to settle, not to mention the production of black mold, which is currently the condition most feared by buyers. (A home with obvious black mold present will cause buyers to shy away or demand a very expensive cleanup.)

In other words, those seemingly harmless piles of debris along the sides of your home can make it more difficult to sell your house and can knock the price down. Remove them and you'll increase the value of your home.

After Clearing the Debris

The moral of this story is to get rid of debris. However, once it's gone, there's also the matter of what to put in its place?

Simply raking and leveling the raw ground can be enough. If you want to get fancy, you can put in stepping stones or a lawn, bushes, or flowers. You can make as big a deal out of the area where once there was debris as you can afford. It will all add to the value of your home.

However, nothing will add more than just getting rid of the debris itself.

$$

Dump the old couches.

Almost everyone has a favorite chair or couch. It's what you sit in when you watch television or listen to the stereo. It's where you go when you want to feel the most comfortable. It's what says home for you.

But not for potential buyers. If you ever watched the television series *Frasier,* you'll remember that Frasier has an apartment filled with designer furniture—except for one old chair that his dad uses. That chair is falling apart and held together with duct tape. It's an eyesore. Yet, it's his dad's favorite place to be and, because of this, Frasier allows it in his otherwise impeccable living room.

But, that's only because Frasier doesn't want to sell his apartment (condo, co-op, or house). If he wanted to sell, that chair would be gone in an instant. The same should hold true for you.

Much of our most beloved furniture is nothing but an eyesore to others. Of course, most of the time we don't really care what others think. When we want to sell, however, it's different.

You may be wondering what difference old, worn, bedraggled furniture would make to a buyer. After all, the buyer is purchasing the house, not the furniture (unless it's thrown in with the sale).

You're right, of course. It shouldn't make any difference to a buyer. But it will.

Buyers have no imagination. What they see is what their mind tells them they'll get. If they see a room with a piece of junk furniture in it, it will tell them that the room is junky and, by association, so is the house. Believe it or not, one eyesore in the living room can cut the buyer's bid.

Get rid of that ugly piece of furniture that you love, and you'll get more money for your house. (You don't need to throw it out—you can store it until you're ready to move it into your next home. Where it will become an eyesore.)

Furniture to Dump by Room

The hardest thing for most of us is to see our home and its belongings with the buyer's eyes. We're sellers, and we see value everywhere, including in our furniture. But buyers see things differently. They look for a reason to knock the price down. Here's a list of some items you may find loveable, but which a buyer could detest, by room:

Living or Family Room

- Old, ragged couch.
- Worn out stuffed chair.
- Worn area rug (particularly old oriental rugs).
- Scuffed and scratched furniture (check the legs).
- Old, decrepit piano.
- Ottoman that the cat/dog sits on and chews.
- Plastic on your furniture (yes, it was intended to keep it looking like new—now it makes it look old and tired).
- Old television set or stereo (the older models look tired and so will the room they're in).
- Cords protruding or hanging from various appliances. It makes the room look like an industrial site.

Dining Room

- Scratched, scuffed, or stained table and chairs (check the legs).

- Dirty, torn, or sun-bleached chair cushions.
- Old hutch or china cabinet with broken glass, stains, scuffs, or scratches. An overstuffed china cabinet contributes to a crowded look, making the room appear smaller.
- Torn, ragged, stained, or dirty area rug or carpet.

Kitchen

- Scratched, scuffed, or stained table and chairs (again, check the legs).
- Dirty, torn, or sun-bleached chair cushions.
- Old fashioned, worn, or torn table cover or placemats.

Bedrooms

- Worn or stained comforter or bed cover.
- Scratched, scuffed, or stained bedroom furniture.
- Torn, ragged, stained, or dirty area rug or carpet.
- Old television set or stereo.
- Clothes strewn about. (This is a no-brainer, but sometimes a word to the wise will help.)

How Do You Replace the Furniture?

It's okay to just get rid of that big couch in your living room. But now you've got a living room without a couch. If you got rid of an old overstuffed chair and a torn area rug, your living room may look rather bare (see the first technique for reasons not to worry so much, here). What do you do to put some furniture back?

It's a truism that buyers like to see a home with some (not a lot) of furniture in it. Get rid of your old loveable (to you) pieces and your rooms may look barren. That can make them look smaller than they are, a definite disadvantage for buyers.

Increasingly, a complete furniture makeover is being done to sell upscale homes. *All* of the old furniture is removed. An interior decorator is hired to come in and determine what new furniture should be obtained and where to place it. Most of the new furniture is rented (you can rent almost anything these days) and in a short time, the entire look and feel of a home's interior can be brightened, sweetened, and made to say, "Buy me!"

An interior makeover can cost many thousands of dollars . . . a month! A less costly approach is to get rid of that one eyesore from each room and then replace it creatively. You might actually rent a couch and chair for a hundred a month. In the bedroom, you can dress up an old bed with a new bedspread. A dining or kitchen table can be disguised under a long, new tablecloth. Legs of furniture can be buffed and polished to hide scuffs, scratches, and stains. You can remove the old television set and you can certainly hide wires that are exposed. Just remove old, worn area rugs and let the flooring underneath show, assuming it's in good condition. If it's not, consider a new and inexpensive area rug. A new rug of even the poorest quality usually looks far better than an older, worn expensive rug.

Dump your old eyesores and make over the interior of your house. You'll be adding value when you sell.

TECHNIQUE **8** $

Replace your home's jewelry.

We all know that putting on fine jewelry makes a person look richer, finer, more desirable. The same thing holds true for a home.

A home's jewelry includes all those metal items that are found on the front. These typically consist of the front door handle, knocker, and lock as well as the ubiquitous light fixture that's found by the front door and even the street numbers. These are the items that dress up the house for a potential buyer, the first things that he or she sees as they prepare to enter.

While it's not really possible to say how much increased value new "jewelry" will add to a home, suffice to say that it will make the home far easier to sell. It could make buyers perceive the home as more upscale (than it would appear without the new items) and therefore more valuable.

The Light Fixture

There is almost always a light fixture right by the front door. It's there for a good reason, to brighten the entranceway so that you don't trip in the dark when you go into the home and to provide light when you fumble for your key.

However, most entrance light fixtures were installed by the original builder. Often the builder, while trying to come up with a nice fixture, was interested in cutting costs. Therefore, while the original fixture may be okay, it's probably not a sparkling piece of home jewelry. Consider replacing it.

This does not mean you need to spend a large sum on a new light fixture. For a hundred dollars or less, you can purchase quite beautiful fixtures. These come in the usual gold, brass, and tarnished brown colors. However, depending on the style of your home, you may want to consider one of the fixtures that come in a variety of metallic colors such as dark green, dark blue, and so on.

Some of these fixtures are no longer made of metal at all, but instead they are made of a strong, inert plastic that readily accepts paint. Recently, while dressing up the jewelry in front of my house, I bought a beautiful but neutral colored plastic fixture and then spray painted it to match the home's trim colors. This made it a unique piece; one that caught the eye and brought many compliments. Instead of just being a ho-hum item that a buyer's eyes would pass over without seeing, it now contributed to selling the property.

These fixtures are hard-wired into the house wiring and if you're not knowledgeable about wiring, be sure you have an electrician install it for you. *Be sure all the power is off before doing any electrical work.*

The Door Handle and Lock

This is what people handle, twist, and push all the time. Therefore, it is understandable that after a few years most door handles and locks begin to get a tarnished, blotchy look. They look well-used, old, distressed. That's not the way you want your home to appear.

Replacing these with new items can be either quite costly, as much as $500 or more, or quite inexpensive, as little as under $50. Why the disparity? It has to do with quality.

There are all sorts of elaborate front door handles and locks that are really made out of cheap metal with an electrostatic coating that gives them a shiny gold, brass, or even silver appearance. Put them in and they'll look great, for a while. Typically, however, after a year or so of use, they turn into that worn item described earlier. My suggestion is that if you're planning to sell your home within the next six months, then by all means consider installing one of these low budget items. They'll look great to the vast majority of buyers.

On the other hand, if you're going to stay in the home for a long time, consider the real thing. These are solid metal, typically brass, often with coatings that deter tarnishing. They will last forever and if they do get tarnished, will quickly clean up to look as good as new. Of course, they cost significantly more.

Installation Problems

It would seem that installing a new front door handle and safety lock would be simple. You just remove the old one and put the new one in. That, after all, is what the packaging frequently says.

Having done it many times, I can assure you that it's not nearly as easy as that. The problem is that sometimes the old holes don't match the new equipment. When that happens, you've got a real problem. You don't want to be drilling new holes in your front door (plugging the old holes so they don't show can be a really difficult chore).

My suggestion is that if this happens, you immediately abandon the project for the moment and return to the new front door handle. Take the measurements of your door (the distance from the center of the holes to the door edge) to the store and see if you can find a new handle and dead-bolt lock that fit. Often, it's just a matter of getting a different brand. Don't try to make one that doesn't fit, work. You'll just get yourself aggravated (and you could mess up your door).

If you can't find one that fits, then consider having a professional install it. Yes, it will cost much more, but the appearance will be well worth it.

Doorknocker or Doorbell

There's always a doorknocker or doorbell. Consider replacing the one that is there with a much nicer one. If it's a doorbell, you can find beautiful replacements for the outside piece for well under $20. If it's a doorknocker, it might cost you as much as $100.

Just consider how the new buyer will feel pulling on that doorknocker and feeling the hard, solid metal or pushing on the new doorbell. Don't underestimate the tactile value here. It can be important.

Note: Front door alerting devices have gone high tech. Today you can buy a combination doorbell, remote television unit. When someone presses the bell, a camera takes his picture and flashes it on a monitor (or television set) inside the house. This setup costs several hundred dollars, however, it's guaranteed to be a conversation piece. While a potential buyer might pooh-pooh it as a, "Who needs that," piece, in the back of that buyer's mind will be a little thought that goes, "Wouldn't that be cool to have!" If nothing else, later in the day after touring a dozen homes, the buyer will remember your house as the one with the remote camera at the front door.

Other Jewelry

Your house may or may not have other jewelry on it, such as:

- *Garage door handle and lock:* Even if your garage door has an electric opener, there still is often a handle. To replace this with a shiny new piece often only costs a few dollars, yet again, it will be noticed.
- *Decorative pieces:* Some homes have religious or decorative pieces. If they look shabby, why not just remove them? If you want them to stay, be sure to clean them up.
- *Transom:* Like the door handle, this gets a lot of use. Often it too can look distressed. However, a transom is not so easily replaced. Often it's an integral part of the door frame. Some polish and elbow grease can do wonders. On the other hand, if your transom is easily removed, why not replace it? The cost is usually minimal.

TECHNIQUE **9**   **$**

Get rid of house odors.

There's a local restaurant that I used to like very much. The food was terrific, the prices were reasonable, and for a time it was very popular.

But when my wife and I were there the last time, right at the front entrance, we couldn't help but notice a strong sulfur smell, the noxious kind that comes from a sewer. (Perhaps a local drain was not functioning properly.) I looked around wrinkling my nose and noticed that another person going in was having the same reaction.

We went inside and had our meal, but it wasn't the same. Somehow that smell outside, even though not present inside, tainted everything. We haven't been back since.

Odors count, in a big way. The primary sense for most mammals is smell. Most of us humans, however, rarely rely on smell, instead we primarily use our eyes to sense the world. Nevertheless, our sense of smell is still strong and primal. A bad odor works as a warning to us at a very deep level—it tells us to stay away from whatever's causing the smell. When potential buyers tour your house, a lingering smell, even at the subconscious level, can be a big negative factor in the decision to purchase and in the amount to offer.

But, you may be saying, my house doesn't smell bad.

Doesn't it? Most homes that are more than a year old have developed an odor of one sort or another. Water leaks, typically in the bathroom and kitchen, work to produce mold that creates a musty odor. Some types of glue and paneling can produce a formaldehyde smell. Even the drains and toilets in our homes can produce smells, although they have traps built in specifically to prevent that from happening. Cooking (and sometimes burning) can give a home an odor. Any moisture underneath carpeting can cause the development of mold which, as noted, produces odor. (This is particularly the case with homes built on cement slabs.)

All of which is to say, it's the rare house that doesn't smell!

Check Your Home's Odors

It's difficult for most of us to smell the odors in our own home. Over time we've simply gotten used to them. The best way to find out if your house has a problem is to ask someone else. Ask someone who will be honest with you. (Many people simply don't like to mention such things.) Try asking a good friend, a neighbor, or a real estate agent.

Unless your house reeks, don't expect them to give you a negative answer. They might say something like, "Yes, I noticed something as I came in, but it's not bad . . . don't worry about it."

Trust me, worry about it. No, this is probably not going to be the biggest factor in a buyer's decision to purchase. But it will be a factor. The more negatives you can change to positives, the better your chances of a fast and profitable sale.

What Can I Do?

Check bathrooms first. The two biggest sources of odors are toilet leaks and leaks under sinks that are hidden in cabinets. Contrary to popular belief, most toilets do not leak at the tank. Rather, they leak at the base where the toilet joins the floor. Underneath the toilet is a wax seal that, if distorted or misaligned, will allow waste from the toilet to seep out onto the floor.

This is one of those chores no one likes, but get down on your hands and knees and smell at the base of the toilet. If you get a strong odor there, chances are your toilet is leaking. Get a plumber to put in a new wax seal.

Also remove all of the things you've got in the cabinet under the sink and look and feel around inside. It should be dust dry. Any moisture or any mold is bad. You'll want to fix the leak and clean it thoroughly (use a very mild solution of bleach and water to get rid of the mold while protecting your skin and eyes) and then paint with an exterior paint that has an antifungal agent.

Finally, look for any signs of mold on surfaces, particularly around the tub or shower. These can usually be scrubbed off.

In the kitchen, the procedure is the same for under the sink. Also check the drains. While a trap should effectively keep sewer odors out, sometimes decaying food will get stuck on the walls of the drain. Usually a solution of vinegar followed by a solution of baking soda will remove the odor at least temporarily.

Odors rising from the floor are much more serious. The floor should always be dust dry. If there's any moisture, mold will form, particularly in carpet backing, and it is almost impossible to get out.

The problem of mold under carpets is usually found in homes built on slabs. The builder should have put an impermeable plastic membrane down beneath the slab before pouring the concrete. The membrane acts as a moisture barrier. No membrane, and moisture will get through. A similar problem can occur in walls where no moisture barrier was placed between the outside and inside walls.

The right cure here is to replace the slab, first putting in a moisture barrier, or to pour a second slab with a moisture barrier in between. However, you could be looking at tens of thousands of dollars of repair work. This is something you may want to take up with the builder of the home. You'll certainly need to disclose the problem to any future buyer.

A short-term solution may be to raise the carpeting and replace any padding that has mold. You can also put drying agents on the floor as well as baking soda to help absorb the odors.

Some real estate agents recommend boiling a pot of spices on the stove when buyers come to look at the house. This gives the home a pleasant aroma as well as driving out any minimal musty smell. However, if there is a real problem, it should be disclosed or resolved.

What about Animal Smells?

If you have a cat or dog that has urinated on the floor, you have a very serious problem. Once the urine has penetrated carpeting or other flooring, it is almost impossible to get the smell out. That smell can be quite strong, even from just a few spots.

Note: I once saw a seller try to cover up the animal smell in a house by always showing the place with the windows open. The people who bought the home, however, were driven out by the urine odor the first week when they closed all the windows and turned on the heat. The buyers sued and eventually the sellers had to spend over $10,000 putting in brand new carpeting and flooring for the buyers.

Thoroughly check all the floors for urine smells, even if it means crawling around on all fours. (Whenever I buy a house, that's exactly what I do—no matter how ridiculous it looks—to discover any hidden odors.)

If you find some odors, replace the carpeting and pad. If there's wood flooring, it may need to be replaced. Cement flooring can sometimes be sealed to keep the odor from rising.

Animal smells can be more than just a negative influence on the buyer. They can be a serious liability issue.

Don't Forget Noise

While we're on the subject of senses, don't forget that other sense, hearing. Noise can drive buyers away. Keep all radios and music players down low or off. If there's street noise, keep the windows closed so the buyers will see that inside the house it's quiet, even if outside it's noisy. The same holds true for other neighborhood noises.

Pay attention to your buyer's sense of smell (and hearing). It will pay big dividends.

TECHNIQUE **10**   **$**

Hang pictures from the masters.

Empty walls make a home look barren, institutional, sort of like a school or even a prison. Empty walls say that the house is unlived in and, to a certain extent, unlivable. When a buyer walks through a home and sees barren walls, subconsciously it can be a turn-off. Besides making the place actually look smaller, it can also make it seem downright unfriendly.

Most of us have a few pictures hanging on our walls. Some of us actually have too many pictures on the walls, thus adding to the clutter. (See Technique 1 about clutter.)

However, few homeowners have pictures that will attract buyers. Too often, we have a garish black silk print, or a highly stylish and colorful modern rendering, or even one of those tedious images that are found in motel rooms.

In short, it's the rare home that has wall coverings that enhance the property and encourage buyers to make better offers.

But, you may be wondering, can the right sort of pictures hanging on the walls actually influence the sale? Aren't we now delving into an area of minimal effect for significant cost? After all, getting really good pictures can be quite expensive, can't it?

I can only report what I (and other real estate agents I've talked with) have seen. The kinds of wall coverings you have can make your home look rich, or shoddy. They can make it look desirable, or stand-offish. In short, what you hang on the walls won't be the deciding factor in whether a buyer decides to make an offer nor for how much. But it can be a significant contributing factor.

What Kind of Pictures Work?

Look for art from painters such as Monet, Renoir, or Degas. These works are uplifting, rich, and also usually make a good impression on most buyers. The works of Van Gogh, while colorful, can be disturbing and should probably be avoided.

What? You say you can't afford $50,000 and up for a painting? What about $35?

Good quality prints of the masters are available in art supply stores as well as in almost all museums. You can purchase a frame for another $25 (some stores offer two for one sales) and, with a little bit of assembling work, you can have the masters hanging on the walls in your home.

You can get wonderful posters from museums that were used to announce an exhibition. Typically, these will have the museum's name, the exhibition's name, and the dates printed on them. In addition to being art, they also suggest that you're an art lover and attend new showings. If nothing else, they are an attention getter and will cause potential buyers to pause or slow down during their tour of your home, a big plus.

How Many Pictures?

If you already have wall hangings that you're proud of, then you should stick with them. However, keep in mind that just as with furniture, the tendency for most of us is to overdo. We tend to be afraid of empty space. Why put only one painting on a wall, when you can put five? The more paintings, the less empty space there is, and that usually makes us feel more comfortable.

But for buyers, it simply looks like clutter. Usually one hanging per wall is maximum (assuming they are fairly good sized). In smaller rooms, one or two per room is plenty. Remember, this is supposed to be an accent, not a dominant feature. It's supposed to help show off the size and feel of the room, not dwarf it by comparison.

Are There Alternative Wall Coverings?

Certainly. Just because you read in this book that the impressionists are in vogue doesn't mean that you must abide by it. You can hang whatever you like, as long as it enhances the home.

I've seen people hang fabrics and rugs on walls. While tapestries are not popular today, in previous times they were the hangings of choice in most upscale homes.

If you opt for an alternative to a painting, be very careful with the colors. We'll discuss using muted colors when you repaint in Technique 32, for now, remember that with a single hanging you need not be so bland. Rather, the hanging can be the accent that brings life and liveliness to the room. Don't be afraid to use a splash of color here and there.

A word to the wise, however. If you're like me, you may have trouble knowing just how much and which colors to use. If that's the case, it's time to call in an expert. Most department stores have interior decorators on call and either for free, or a small fee (they're hoping you'll buy from them) will send them to your home to suggest floor coverings, furniture, and in this case, wall hangings. If they're any good, they'll have an eye for color and will be able to suggest what to hang on your walls to enhance your rooms.

What about Window Coverings?

It's common to have shades, curtains, drapes, or blinds on windows. Since the window areas make up about 15 percent of most rooms, that's a lot of wall covering to think about.

Rather than go out and try to buy new window coverings to enhance the rooms of your house, remove all but the simplest that you have. Remember, you want to bring as much light into the rooms as possible. Hence, keeping the windows clear is your best choice.

You may have some window coverings, such as wood blinds, which are an asset and which will add value to your home. My suggestion is that you open them. On the other hand, remove any heavy drapes, curtains, or other coverings that obscure the wood blinds. While most buyers will consider blinds an asset, they will discount all the other window coverings. They will simply see them as something to be discarded once they move in.

Further, most window coverings tend to be massive and shrink the appearance of rooms. You're probably better off without them.

Let a few paintings and wall and window coverings add the color your rooms need and enhance your home's value.

Techniques That Will Improve Neighborhood Values

TECHNIQUE **11**   **$$$$$**

Take neighborhood action.

As you probably already know, the watchwords that every-one in real estate lives (and dies) by are, "Location, location, location!"

When you buy, you are wisely urged to purchase in the very best location you can afford, because that will result in greater profits when you sell. Everyone knows (or should know) that buyers purchase neighborhoods before homes. Indeed, one of the first questions most buyers ask real estate agents is, "Where are the best areas I can afford?"

What if you already own your home and the location isn't as good as it might be? The purchase decision was made long ago. Maybe this was the only house you could afford at that time. Perhaps you fell in love with the design and didn't pay attention to the surrounding homes. Or maybe the neighborhood changed for the worse.

What now? Do you just have to live with a bad neighborhood, and take a big hit when you try to sell? Or is there something you can do?

Conventional Thinking

If you ask the average person (or real estate agent) for techniques to help improve the location of your house, chances are they will look at you as if you're daft.

Traditionally, once you're in a location it's like a marriage, you're stuck with it for good or for bad. After all, while you have almost complete control of your own property, the location is determined by other people's property . . . and, presumably, you have no control over that.

No way to improve your location? Indeed. As it turns out, there are many, many things you can do to improve the location of your home. (Don't listen to those who pooh-pooh this.) Remember, improving the location can be one of the fastest ways to improve the value of your property.

Think about it. If your house is selling for $100,000 less than the same house across town in a better neighborhood, what would it take for your neighborhood to become better? Even if you make just a minimal improvement in the neighborhood, with a national housing shortage and with people looking for bargains every day, buyers would beat a path to your door. As homes around you begin to sell for more, the value of your property would climb steadily.

Unconventional Thinking

Okay, I've got your attention, but you've still got a healthy amount of skepticism. After all, logic dictates that you can't change your home's location.

Right. You can't move your house (at least not very easily). But, as those in advertising know, it's not the steak that sells; it's the sizzle. Perception is everything. If your neighborhood is perceived as better than it was, prices will go up. Your "new" location will be the same old one only dressed in finer clothes. You're going to give your neighborhood a makeover!

Not easily done, I'm sure you're saying. No, it's not as easy as simply putting your house up for sale at your present location and accepting 10, 20, perhaps 50 percent less in value than you'd get if the neighborhood was nicer.

On the other hand, if you're anxious to improve the value of your home (translate this to make more money), then maybe you're willing to do something to make that happen.

What You Need to Improve Your Neighborhood

1. *Energy:* Nobody else is going to do this for you. You have to get off the dime and do it yourself. That's not to say you need do it *all* by yourself. But for every engine there's a spark plug, for every snowball there's a starter, for every . . . you get the idea. You need to be the one to initiate action. But just remember, once the engine's running and the snowball's moving, they'll continue on their way gathering more and more energy. You just need to get the action started.

2. *Determination:* There will be those who will scoff. There will be those who won't want to do anything to improve their, and your, neighborhood. Until you start to get some results, there may be times when you feel like you're standing alone yelling into a hurricane. But, if you persevere, you'll get the rewards, usually in a much higher price for your property.

3. *Time:* Rome wasn't built in a day and neighborhood improvement usually doesn't happen overnight. That's why it's a good idea to start now, before you need to sell your home. If you start a year or even several years earlier, it will all be to the better. Even if you're not thinking of selling, now is still the time to prepare for that eventuality and get started improving your neighborhood.

You've just listed your home? You need to see your neighborhood improve by next Tuesday!

Surprisingly, sometimes critical changes can occur almost overnight. We'll consider slower changes in the following techniques, but here's a true example of an instant makeover.

Many years ago, before I got heavily involved in real estate, I bought a home in a working class neighborhood in the San Fernando valley of Los Angeles. It was our (my wife and kids and my) first home and we really didn't pay much attention to, "location, location, location." Instead, we were concerned mainly with getting into the biggest house that we could afford for our family, regardless of where it was.

We moved in. We soon discovered that the neighbor directly across the street never mowed her lawn or cut her shrubs. She often let debris gather on her lawn. Her house looked a mess. She was a single woman with three children who, apparently, had her hands full.

We tried to look the other way and tolerate it. My next door neighbor wasn't so understanding and regularly complained, but nothing came of it.

After two years, we decided to move to a better neighborhood. We wanted to put our home up for sale. We called several real estate agents who told us that our home would probably sell, but only if we charged 20 percent less than it would be worth in a better "location." That neighbor across the street was driving our property's value down.

So, in a neighborly fashion, I went across the street and said that I was concerned about the condition of her property and was there anything I could do to help out? She was angry, at first, that I had brought up the issue, but when I emphasized the word "help," she said she simply didn't have the money or the capability of mowing her lawn. (She only had a push mower.)

I volunteered to pay a boy to come in once a week to mow the lawn. Then, along with another neighbor, we volunteered to give the front of her house a new coat of paint and to put in some shrubs, if she would pay for materials. She said she didn't have the money to spare, so we paid for the materials as well (it was only a hundred dollars apiece, or so).

Within a few weeks, the front of her place looked like a dollhouse. The lawn was nice and neat and the shrubs were manicured.

I put my house up for sale and it sold quickly at close to list price. Of course, I told the buyers about my across-the-street mowing arrangement (the price of which I was splitting with my neighbor) and although they seemed puzzled, I was fairly sure they would quickly get the hang of it.

The moral to this story is that you can dramatically and quickly improve the value of your property by getting rid of a neighborhood eyesore. You can often do this in a friendly way and for very little cost.

You do, however, have to handle the situation creatively. And you have to be willing to put yourself out a bit. Remember, if you don't do it, no one else will.

TECHNIQUE **12**   **$$$**

Push your Homeowners' Association.

Got a neighborhood problem that's lowering the value of your home? Is there someone (or two or three) whose front yard is weed-strewn and ragged? Does a neighbor's house desperately need painting? Is someone's driveway cracked and coming up?

Hard to handle? If you have a homeowners' association (HOA), you may have the perfect mechanism to take care of the problems.

A great many developments across the country have homeowners' associations. This doesn't just include condominium developments, but also includes single-family homes. In some cases, these organizations are active and work hard to maintain a good looking neighborhood. However, in a great many cases, over the years the HOAs have become inactive, particularly if there isn't a community-owned property, such as a clubhouse or swimming pool. People get tired of serving, there are few issues, and the HOA simply seems to fade away, often run almost entirely by a management service, if run at all.

If you have an HOA as part of your development, then it is a natural focus for improving the neighborhood. It usually has the tools to handle problem homeowners and to turn things around. Get the HOA behind you to improve the value of the entire neighborhood. (We'll see what to do without a HOA in the next technique.)

How Do I Get My Homeowners' Association to Help?

You'll know if you're part of an active HOA. There will be meetings you'll be asked to attend, notices of various activities will be sent around, and most important, you'll be asked to pay a monthly fee. (We'll discuss what to do shortly if your HOA is inactive.)

In theory, an active HOA should already be on top of homeowners who do not keep up their property. Typically there's an architectural committee that checks the neighborhood a couple of times a year and contacts homeowners whose homes and yards need care.

But often, even with an active HOA, there's little incentive to prod a recalcitrant homeowner who refuses to clean up, paint, or whatever. Typically the HOA will send a few notices and then, perhaps, impose a fine. However, seldom is much done to enforce the fine and the wayward homeowner and dilapidated property continue on as before.

If that's the case, then it is up to you to prod the HOA into action. Remember, the squeaky wheel gets the oil. You need to be the squeaky wheel to the HOA.

How to Get Action Out of Your HOA

1. Attend HOA Board meetings regularly (they are typically held once a month or less).
2. Ask to be put on the agenda (usually by calling or writing the president or manager before the meeting).
3. Review the rules. Usually they are quite specific about property upkeep. Know the exact wording and location of the rules that apply.
4. Speak up against a homeowner who is neglecting his or her property. Demand that the Board take action as required under their own rules. Point out that the Board itself could be liable for legal action against it for refusing to follow its own rules.

5. Volunteer to be part of a committee to look into what action to take.

No, you may not win any popularity contests. But, you'll get a lackadaisical Board to sit up and pay attention. When the Board shows determination, things usually get done. The Board can:

- Send clean-up demands.
- Fine the homeowner for refusing to clean up as demanded.
- Put a lien on the property (in some states) or go to small claims court to enforce the fines.
- Begin a lawsuit against the homeowner.

Usually what happens is that as soon as the Board takes effective action against one homeowner who's let his or her property go downhill, all the other homeowners who have done the same thing take notice. Suddenly there is a snowball effect. Almost overnight you'll begin seeing your neighbors planting flowers and shrubs, putting in new lawns, painting, fixing driveways, and so on. The turnaround can happen quickly. You'll also see this change reflected in a higher valuation for your property.

What If I Have an Inactive HOA?

If there's no entity out there collecting dues and enforcing architectural control, how would you even know if you have an HOA?

HOA information should have been given to you when you purchased and moved into your home. Check the documents you received—you probably have them saved in some corner of your garage.

Look for the conditions, covenants, and restrictions (CC&Rs). They can provide for the creation of an HOA. Also check for a set of bylaws or rules under which the HOA operates. As a last resort, check with your county planning department. They should have records of all developments with HOAs.

If your neighborhood has an inactive HOA, then it's up to you to activate it. Don't even think about trying to create an HOA if one doesn't exist. It would take an enormous amount of effort on your part to create such an association and then it would have to be voted in by almost all (if not all) of the homeowners. If you don't have an HOA, just move on to the next technique.

Here's an almost true story (the names have been changed). A friend of mine, Cathy, bought a home without paying much attention to the neighborhood. Once living there, she realized that many of the homes were just plain shabby and their yards were in terrible condition.

She talked to a few of the homeowners, but they saw the neighborhood as basically run down and didn't see any reason to put any effort into their individual homes. Something more powerful than just one person was needed to get things turned around.

So Cathy investigated and discovered that 20 years ago, when the neighborhood had been built, the CC&Rs provided for the creation of an HOA. There were even preliminary by-laws. However, the HOA had no real property (no recreation facility, no pool, not even any walking trails), so it had never formally gotten going.

Cathy saw this as an opportunity. She talked to as many neighbors as she could buttonhole on a weekend and got four others to agree to serve on a Board. Then she wrote and cir-culated a newsletter (actually just a flyer) talking about the advantages of activating the HOA, the most important of which was getting the neighborhood cleaned up and looking better.

Cathy checked with an attorney to be sure she was using the right procedure, then she and the other four would-be Board members held an election.

As it turned out, just the activity caused several of the neighbors with run-down places to get out and work on their lawns and landscaping. A few more began painting their homes.

At the election, only those who cared about improving the neighborhood voted and soon Cathy was on the Board. Its first action was to impose dues. Since there were about 250 homes and the dues were only $10 a month, payable annually (and since she sent out flyers to everyone explaining that the money would be used to enforce architectural improvements in the neighborhood), the Board soon had a war chest of over $25,000. (The few who complained about the minimal dues were mostly those whose properties were in bad shape.)

The Board decided to notify all the homeowners whose properties were run down that they needed to improve them, and began fining those who didn't, about two dozen.

About half of these complied. But the house in the worst shape, owned by Sam, remained so. Sam was outraged; he refused to clean up or to pay the fines. He denied the Board's right to insist he clean up his property.

After six months of going nowhere, Cathy and the Board hired an attorney to bring suit again Sam. The legal preparations cost the Board about $2,500.

The most important outcome was that Sam was forced to hire his own attorney, who informed him that it was a legally constituted Board that did have the right of architectural control. It would be far easier for Sam simply to clean up his yard and paint his house, than to fight. So he did.

It took three more lawsuits, none of which got further than Sam's did, before every house in the neighborhood looked shipshape. Within a year, Cathy's neighborhood did an about face. Real estate agents, who once spoke of it as a declining area or as a shoddy neighborhood, began directing buyers to it. Prices began moving up.

The upshot of this story is that by the time Cathy sold, six years later, hers was a top neighborhood and she got top dollar.

Can You Really Do It?

Of course you can. Remember, often all that's needed is a spark plug, one person to take responsibility, to get the ball rolling.

Of course, Cathy was in a neighborhood that had an inactive HOA. Her course would have been much easier if the HOA had been active. However, she could still have done much even if there was no HOA around. See the next technique.

TECHNIQUE **13**   **$$$$**

Form a Neighborhood Action Committee.

A neighborhood action committee (NAC) is what you can use to transform your neighborhood if you don't have a homeowners' association.

Remember the old saying, "There's strength in numbers." When it comes to getting a neighborhood turned around, that's absolutely true.

In Technique 11 we saw how an individual can get a single neighbor to improve the appearance of a property. But, what if there are a dozen or two dozen nearby homes that are run-down. Can you as an individual do much about this? Probably not.

If you have an HOA, active or inactive, you can use it to get things improved as we saw in the last technique. But, what if you don't have an HOA?

Even without an HOA, if you organize your neighbors, you have a great opportunity to get positive things done. Of course, there are some big limitations with a NAC when compared to an HOA. With an HOA, you may have legal remedies to enforce neighborhood conformity. On the other hand, a NAC can only suggest, prod, and help. However, if done correctly, that's often enough.

How Can a NAC Make Big Changes?

Here are some of the things that a NAC can do:

1. It can determine what's needed to improve a neighborhood, whether that be clean-up, landscaping, paint, child-care, or whatever.

2. It can one-on-one and at meetings present information on home valuations and why they are likely to increase if the neighborhood moves up.

3. It can actually do some of the fix-up/clean-up work itself.

4. It can gain the respect of owners who are more likely to appreciate the visit of a NAC member than an individual homeowner. Many owners (not all) will feel peer pressure to improve their properties.

5. It can more easily secure the help of charities, government agencies, and other bodies. (See the following techniques for more on this.)

How Do I Form a NAC?

As I said in Technique 11, it takes a spark plug to get the car running. Unless there's already someone out there organizing things who you can help, you'll need to be the initiator yourself. You'll need to begin contacting as many of your neighbors as you can.

If you live on a block, talk to those people who are most active in the neighborhood. Often it's the Little League coach or soccer coach. It might be the homeowners who organized the block party last summer. It could be the guys who go bowling or the gals who have an investment or garden club. Determine what's out there by talking to people and then take advantage of existing relationships.

Usually it begins with a meeting held in your (or someone else's) home one evening. Get as many of your neighbors to attend as you can. Offer to buy the pizza and drinks. Be sure to get those leaders we talked about earlier, the ones who help with kids' sports, who organize block parties, who are generally well known.

Before the meeting, get some accurate statistics. From real estate agents, find out what the average price of a home in your area is. That's done by getting a list of sales going back over the last year or so, adding up all the sales prices and then dividing by the number of sales. That will tell you what the average home in your neighborhood sells for. Assuming all the homes are similar, it should give you a good gauge to judge valuations.

Then, with the help of real estate agents, determine two other neighborhoods that have similar housing, but which are in much better shape. Go through the same procedure. You should see that the better neighborhoods have much higher average prices.

Note: Real estate agents should be very pleased to help you. After all, in getting to know you and your friends, they're planting the seeds for future listings and sales.

At the meeting, after establishing rapport (by joking about the weather, or the latest on Letterman or whomever people are watching on the tube), launch into your observations that the houses look shabby. Don't mention anyone in particular, because they may be at the meeting and may not appreciate being publicly identified. Rest assured, those who are guilty know who they are. (Also, don't broach the three taboo topics: sex, politics, and religion. You want bonding, not fracturing.)

Once everyone agrees that the neighborhood looks bad, which shouldn't be too hard to get agreement on, pull out your statistics. Show that the average house in your neighborhood sells for $xxx,xxx less than virtually the same house across town. It's the neighborhood that makes the difference. Make the point that if your neighborhood looked as good as the other, each home owner would stand to add $xx,xxx in equity to their property. That will get everyone thinking if nothing else does.

Finally, don't let everybody agree and then wander away. Once you've generated momentum, stick with it. Explain how the neighborhood can be transformed by working together. Talk about forming a NAC. Do it that night. Get everyone to contribute some money to help with the organization, even if it's only $10 apiece. Nothing cements commitment to an organization like having paid dues into it. Get a Board (president, vice-president, secretary, and treasurer). Decide on your first course of action. Maybe there's one house that needs help. Make it your NAC's first project.

Do What It Takes

I have a friend, Jimmy, who formed a NAC and had several serious problems to deal with. In his area, many of the homes were owned by absentee owners. In other words, they were rented to tenants. Many of these were rundown.

Jimmy and his NAC felt this was the place to start. If they could get the rentals improved, then they believed the owner-occupants would be quick to jump on board and fix up their properties.

Their first course of action was to talk with the tenants. Some agreed to help out, mow lawns, do extra watering, remove trash. But none would agree to pay for new plantings or painting. After all, it wasn't their property.

Jimmy's committee's next move was to talk with the owners. Some were in town. Others were out of town. He contacted them in person, by phone, by e-mail, and by fax. The message: There was a movement afoot to improve the neighborhood. This would increase property values which meant that the owner could sell for more in the long run, and perhaps rent for more in the short run.

One thing about investor/owners, absentee or not: Money talks. The owners to a person agreed to invest, at least minimally, in their properties from new paint to new lawns and shrubs, to removing trash to fixing driveways. Many of the tenants who had refused to help out by painting, now participated . . . after all, the owner was paying for the paint!

The neighborhood movement began to show results. Dozens of homes were simultaneously being improved. Jimmy now went to the other owners and explained about his NAC. He got them to join and to contribute. Dues were now up to $50, but people didn't complain, because they saw results. Individual homeowners began improving their properties as well.

Of course, there are always holdouts. But Jimmy's NAC had the financial means (as well as the muscle power) to go in and paint the front of a property themselves. They fixed windows and screens. They trimmed shrubs. Almost always, once the property was fixed up, the owners maintained them.

Within only a few short months, Jimmy's neighborhood was visibly turning around. Soon new buyers came in, anxious to take advantage of the low prices found in a "turn-around" neighborhood. And, of course, prices began moving up.

It took a NAC to do it.

One person can hardly make a big difference. But one person leading a crowd can make a huge difference.

TECHNIQUE **14**   **$$**

Get allied with a painter/paint store.

Most of us are blind to color. That's different from being color blind. What I mean is that while we appreciate color, we don't really see it as influential. It's just the way things, in this case houses, are painted. One color is as good as another, as long as we avoid wild colors such as purple or bright mustard. No big deal, right?

Actually, the color of the home, as well as the condition of the paint, is quite important when it comes to valuations. There are "older" colors that detract from a neighborhood's value and "newer" colors that add to it. Perhaps an example will help.

I currently live in a California neighborhood where the homes are about 30 years old. A Spanish theme is pretty much consistent throughout the area and originally all of the homes were painted off-white beige with chocolate brown trim.

To my untrained eye, it seemed fine. True, many of the homes looked a bit dingy because they hadn't been painted in a decade or more. But, I figured the color itself was fine. Boy, was I wrong!

I'm on the Board of our homeowners' association and a new member, Sarah, happened to be a designer who knew colors. At the Board meetings, she began talking about the dated colors of our neighborhood. How buyers were shying away because of them. After hearing this several times, I finally raised my hand and timidly asked, "What do you mean dated colors? How can a color have a date?"

I then received a fairly extensive lecture on the history of colors, especially that of house colors. It turns out that every decade or so, builders of new homes change the colors of their buildings to keep up with the latest trends in design. They use different main colors and up to two or three levels of new trim colors. For example, Sarah pointed out, several decades ago, dark colors were in. "When our tract was built, everyone loved beige and dark brown. Virtually every tract built during that era was the same color. However, 10 years later the colors changed to lighter browns. Then came a lot of creams, whites, and pinks. Most recently, tracts in our area are featuring greens and blues."

I simply hadn't observed this. But, I was no slouch. So the next chance I had, I drove to several nearby neighborhoods and observed just the colors. She was absolutely right. You could peg the decade the homes were built by the colors used. Any buyer would immediately know a new neighborhood from an older one by the color of the majority of its homes. Our neighborhood was dating itself by continuing to have houses painted beige trimmed with dark brown. The homes looked old and tired, even those few that had recently been repainted in the same colors!

It was a revelation. At the next Board meeting, I brought up what I had learned and now other Board members decided to see for themselves. Soon, we all agreed that our neighborhood had a problem. We decided to get everyone to update the colors of their homes.

As you might guess, this was no simple thing. It costs around $2,500 to $3,000 at minimum to have the exterior of a home painted and getting homeowners to spend that much money when they all have other bills to pay can be quite difficult.

Nevertheless, led by Sarah, we embarked on a color education program. It was designed to teach both why colors made a big difference, and to get neighbors to repaint their homes. Here's how it worked.

Note: In our example, this was more easily done because the homeowners' association was already in place. However, it can just as well be done through a NAC (see Technique 13) or even just as a group of concerned neighbors.

Color Education Program

1. *Connect with a paint/design center.* You may have the old-fashioned concept (I did) that a paint store is simply a place to go and buy a gallon of this or that color paint. But today, many paint stores are far more. They are actually design centers. Paint companies are very aware of the changing face of neighborhood colors and they have all sorts of color palettes available. (Benjamin Moore is a leader here.) A good paint store will have someone with design skills who can help you pick colors that are modern and that will fit well with the design of neighborhood homes. They'll even come out to look at the neighborhood and give an assessment. Sarah connected with just such a store.

2. *Set up a color palette.* The color designer from the store came out and put together a book of colors that would be suitable. These included the main colors for the home plus two levels of coordinated trim colors. These were all colors that were modern and that worked together. If you wanted to paint your home, all you had to do was come down and pick out a combination that you liked. The result would look terrific. After the paint palette was created, Sarah talked it up to our homeowner members and then had it displayed at an association meeting. Everyone liked the new colors.

3. *Get a big discount.* You can pay retail or you can pay wholesale. The difference is about 25 percent to 40 percent—that is no small amount. Sarah told the paint store that because they had created the neighborhood palette (and their name was on every color sample), they were likely to get business from most if not all of the homeowners. This, after all, is why they did the work in the first place. But she then pointed out that she could guarantee almost all of the business, *if* the paint store would come up with a big discount. They did, 25 percent off most paints, 40 percent off on others. On a $20 gallon of paint, that was a $5 savings. If the house needed 40 gallons of paint, the savings was $200. This was a significant savings. Sarah then broadcast the news, via our HOA cable channel, that the savings were available.

4. *Connect with a painter.* Finally, Sarah connected with one of the better local painters and got him to also give a discount. He would agree to cut his price by 30 percent for homeowners who agreed to have their homes painted within six months. That meant that instead of costing $2,500 to $3,000 to get a home painted, it now cost about $1,750 to $2,100—a huge savings. Needless to say, nearly half the homeowners, those who understood why changing color was important, signed up.

Within six months, our neighborhood looked totally different. It was more cheery and colorful. It seemed a better place to live. And those homeowners who hadn't changed their home's color were pressured by their neighbors to do so. No, we still don't have 100 percent compliance, but it's close. And the neighborhood looks like a totally new place.

But what about the bottom line? Have prices moved up?

It's hard to quantify how much the new paint contributed since prices are moving up anyhow. However, our neighborhood certainly seems to have better price increases than other neighborhoods of similar vintage, but with older colors. Homes in our area most certainly sell faster.

All of which is to say that color does count. You can make a big difference in your home's value by working to modernize the colors of your neighborhood.

TECHNIQUE **15**   **$$**

Go after graffiti.

Nobody I know likes graffiti on their property . . . or anywhere in their neighborhood. (I suspect that teenage rebellion against the adult world of property owners is one of the primary motives of the aspiring artists who put graffiti up.)

There's good reason for not wanting graffiti around—it lowers neighborhood values. When buyers see graffiti in a neighborhood in which they are looking to buy, they often turn around and look elsewhere. Graffiti means that there are rebellious kids running loose, damaging property in the area. It can also be an indication of more serious gang activity and increased crime. Why buy in such an area?

As a result, in areas that have graffiti, property values tend to be depressed and even to go down. Certainly they don't increase as fast as in areas that are graffiti free.

But what can you do about graffiti? Isn't it just a stage that neighborhood kids go through? Isn't it a matter of just waiting and it will eventually go away on its own?

Actually, it's not often the neighborhood kids who put up the graffiti. It's usually the kids from other neighborhoods. Waiting for it to go away on its own may so depress neighborhood values that they might never recover.

If you're in a neighborhood in which there is a great deal of graffiti, you'll probably want to take action to remove it to improve the value of your home.

TECHNIQUES THAT WILL IMPROVE NEIGHBORHOOD VALUES

Getting Rid of Graffiti

I have a friend, Jack, who lives in a suburb of Phoenix who had to deal with graffiti in his neighborhood. When he bought his property, a corner lot with a long fence along one side street, he didn't notice any problem. But one day, after about a year of ownership, he came home to discover that his entire fence was covered with graffiti. And it was on other nearby fences and even on the walls of some homes.

Jack wasn't sure who had done it. But, he was sure he didn't want it. So that evening he got a can of paint and repainted his fence. That might have been the end of it. Except that his neighbors didn't do the same thing. Rather, they left the graffiti up.

A few weeks later, Jack awoke to discover more graffiti on his fence. And a few more neighbors had it on their property as well. He got another gallon of paint and covered his fence over. A few weeks later and a repeat performance with more homes affected.

Jack realized that it wasn't just his problem. It was a neighborhood problem. If the entire neighborhood got out there and removed it, chances are the artists who put it up would be discouraged and would go elsewhere. But as long as some of his neighbors tolerated it, it would likely come back . . . and grow.

So, he organized a NAC (see Technique 13) specifically to deal with graffiti. He called as many of his neighbors in as he could reach to have a discussion. He also called in the public affairs officer of his local police department to give them some information.

The public affairs officer explained that there were some gangs in the area and also some teenage kids who were simply freelancing. He offered to have the police patrol the area more often to see if they could pick up the kids. "But," he said, "it is up to the property owners to make the neighborhood as unfriendly to the graffiti artists as possible." That meant covering up their work as soon as it went up. Nothing discourages a graffiti artist more than to see their work erased as soon as it's created.

It turned out that the other property owners were as upset about the graffiti as Jack. They just didn't know what to do about it. Now they did. They went home and repainted. For those few neighbors who couldn't, or weren't willing to paint over the graffiti on their walls by themselves, Jack and his supporters did it for them (of course, obtaining their permission first).

Almost overnight *all* the neighborhood graffiti was gone. A week later the police reported picking up two individuals with spray cans in the area who were attempting to put graffiti on a fence.

The graffiti did pop up a couple of times again over the next few months. But the neighbors' efforts paid off and for the most part it stayed away. Jack had made a serious contribution to increasing neighborhood values as well as improving the value of his own property.

About Graffiti

It's important to understand that graffiti can and does occur in almost all neighborhoods regardless of ethnic makeup or property values. It's just that in the better neighborhoods, the owners remove it immediately and, thus, discourage its further use. That's what helps make these better neighborhoods.

Also, neighborhoods get reputations very quickly among real estate agents and buyers. Those where graffiti is removed quickly by owners banding together are known as strong neighborhoods, good places to live. Those where the neighbors don't work together (usually because there's no spark plug to organize them), are known as weak neighborhoods, sometimes dangerous places to live.

If you have a fence or a wall that seems to attract graffiti on a regular basis, it may be worthwhile to pay a little more for one of the several types of paint that are graffiti resistant. These paints, available at your local paint store, are constituted in such a way that the paint from many spray cans simply won't adhere well, but will run.

Further, you may want to keep extra paint available so that when the graffiti artists hit, you can quickly go out and repaint with the same color. Too often an owner will repaint over graffiti with a color different than the original on the wall. This can look almost as bad as the graffiti itself. (This is particularly the case when it's been some time since the wall was originally painted.)

Be wary of taking individual action against graffiti artists. This is the domain of the police. The last thing you want to do is to organize your neighborhood into some sort of vigilante group whose action might result in someone getting hurt. Your job here is painting over the problem. Not trying to deal directly with those who are perpetrating it.

TECHNIQUE **16**   **$$$**

Go after blighters.

Blighters are industrial or commercial property owners who allow their sites to become eyesores. You've undoubtedly seen this in some unfortunate neighborhoods. There's a factory close by and the fences around the factory are in bad shape. There may be weeds and sometimes abandoned vehicles and dumped garbage in unused areas.

Or, there may be a shopping center that has its lights focused not on its parking lot, but on the houses next door. Or a strip mall that has customers parking up and down residential streets so there are no places for the homeowners' guests to park.

The list is almost endless. This is not to say, however, that all industrial and commercial neighbors are eyesores. Some are very careful to maintain the character of the neighborhood and thus enhance both its and their value. It's those who really don't care about their residential neighbors that we're concerned with here, those who cause local property values to degenerate.

What Can You Do?

If there's a site near your home, or in your neighborhood, that you feel is causing a problem, find out who owns (or manages) the property and speak to them about the problem. Often a one-on-one meeting will do the trick. It may turn out that the owner or manager of the commercial or industrial site simply isn't aware of the problem. Once made aware of it, he or she may see that it's cleaned up and taken care of immediately.

Only one visit may be necessary. Never assume that the person in a position to take care of the problem knows that it exists. They may not.

On the other hand, they may be aware and simply not care. Now, that is a different story. Here's an example of how one person, Vickie, took care of such a problem.

Vickie bought a home at a discount price because it was located on the same street as a shopping center whose primary tenant was a large grocery store. Vickie's new house was across the street from the center.

She knew that there would be some noise and night lighting from the stores and that was taken into account in the discounted price. However, she was not prepared for the mess that the center created on its side of the street.

It was fall when she moved in and the grass belt between the center's sidewalk and the street was dirt. However, after the winter rains, grass began growing there, as well as on a dirt strip on the shopping center. The grass was not cut or maintained. Further, the grocery store would often leave garbage out at night in the area and that would attract stray animals, a real nuisance.

Vickie knew she had a problem. She also knew that if this continued, she had paid too much for her home. (The previous owners had disclosed that there were problems from the shopping center, but Vickie assumed they would be just a little bit of light at night and some additional noise, not what she got.)

So Vickie went to see the grocery store manager who referred her to the shopping center owner. He received her pleasantly enough and told her he'd certainly take care of the problem. But, he did nothing. After three visits, Vickie came to the conclusion that the man had no intention of doing anything. It simply wasn't an important issue to him.

While Vickie's house was the most impacted because it was right across the street, the shopping center's problem affected the entire neighborhood and drew down values. So Vickie asked a dozen nearby homeowners to come over to her house to discuss it. It wasn't exactly a NAC, but it was a group of those homeowners closest to the shopping center and most affected.

Someone suggested that Vickie go down to City Hall and see if they would do something. The homeowners all signed a petition and Vickie took it to the building department, which said it had no jurisdiction over the matter since it was outside the structure.

She took it to the planning department, which said it would ask the owner to do something. A few weeks later, she got a copy of a letter directed at the shopping center's owner asking him to clean up the problem. He had the weeds mowed, once.

She went to the health department and complained about the garbage. A few weeks later, she got a copy of another letter asking the owner to see that all garbage was placed in appropriate containers. The owner did nothing.

Vickie went back and complained to the health department again and to the planning department after the weeds grew back. A few more letters went out, but no action was taken.

Vickie was about to give up. She called another meeting. One of the residents suggested they hire an attorney. But another said he had been forced to do that a few years ago and it had cost him over $10,000 and he wasn't happy with the outcome. None of the neighbors indicated that they were willing to put up that kind of money. So the meeting fell apart with no clear direction about what to do next. One neighbor commiserated with Vickie saying that it had been that way since the shopping center was built. They just had to live with it. So Vickie did.

Then, a few months later, she got a letter from the city indicating that the shopping center owner wanted to put up a new sign in front. There was going to be a public hearing. All neighboring property owners were invited to attend.

Realizing that payback time had come, Vickie called together her group of 14 homeowners. They all attended the meeting and all spoke condemning the shopping center owner for not taking care of his property. If he couldn't even handle mowing weeds and cleaning up garbage, how could he handle taking care of a new sign?

There's power in numbers. Now she and her group were talking to the planning commission, not some assistant in the office. And they heard.

They granted the shopping center owner his new sign, specifying that he must maintain the lawn at the side of his property and that he must maintain appropriate garbage containers surrounded by a new fence. Because of past abuses, he had to fund an account overseen by the city to make sure it was done.

Needless to say, the shopping center owner was angry. But he had brought it on himself. He had to install a watering system and hire a gardener. He had to put up a nice brick fence (under a building permit) to conceal the garbage. And he had to do it before he could put up his big new sign. Certainly he complied.

Will It Work for You?

If sweet talk doesn't work, flexing your muscle usually will. If there's one thing that commercial and industrial property owners need every year or so, it's a permit to update their property, their sign, their driveways, and so on. When that happens, it gives nearby property owners leverage.

However, you have to be ready to go. There is no time to wonder if you should attend the public meetings or if you should speak to your neighbors. It's a call to action. You, too, can do what Vickie did. (And it immediately improved the value of her property.)

TECHNIQUE **17**   **$$$**

Get city hall on your side.

Sometimes you can improve your neighborhood simply by working to be sure that it moves up, rather than down. Changes can be for the worse as well as for the better.

For example, a developer may want to put a strip mall on a street near the heart of your development. It would detract from the residential character of your neighborhood and, over time, would keep your property values from rising.

Or a company may want to site a factory on bare land at the edge of your development. Again, having an industrial use that close could adversely affect your property values.

Or, as in a situation that recently affected a friend of mine, a builder wanted to erect new homes on land that had been designated as "open space" in a master plan. Removing the open space would increase the density of the area, take away its natural beauty, and keep nearby property values from rising.

To improve the value of your property in all of these cases requires taking action. It usually means going before a planning commission or city council to forcefully state your position against the new development. Just doing nothing and hoping things will fall into place usually results in the change for the worst going through.

How to Prevent the Downgrading of Your Neighborhood

1. *Be alert.* Almost always there will be some indication that change is coming. Hopefully, it will be a public notice sent to you, but not always. Sometimes, you have to look for a notice posted on land. Other times, it will be

surveyors staking out a property. Yet other times, it could be an article in a local newspaper. Investigate and find out what is planned.

2. *Get organized.* Form a NAC or at least alert other property owners that there's something afoot. By yourself you'll be crying in the wilderness. Having a dozen neighbors show up at a planning commission hearing, angry and ready to speak shows political clout.

3. *Observe deadlines.* Nothing gets done entirely in private. At some point, there's a public hearing. Usually there are opportunities for written and vocal input. Find out when the deadlines are for these and be sure your input is there, whether written or vocal.

4. *Learn your rights.* It might mean spending several hundred dollars to hire a good attorney to tell you how to block the proposed new development. It will be money well spent.

5. *Get public support.* Don't overlook the power of the press. And don't forget that newspapers love to report a fight— that is news. Call the editor of your local paper and tell them that neighbors are incensed about a new development. Invite a reporter to a NAC or neighborhood group meeting. Paint signs and protest in front of the development. You might get your picture on the front page and that will carry even more political weight.

Plan a Long Fight

My friend's "war" against development of new housing can be instructive. Carey's neighborhood was 20 years old. When it was built, it was in a natural valley surrounded by small hills. The hills were left untouched and sported wild flowers, hiking trails, and wildlife. While neighboring areas became congested with high density homes, Carey's remained open. The hillsides were the best asset of the area.

However, a developer correctly surmised that if he could build bigger homes on the hills overlooking Carey's development, he could reap huge profits. The new homes would have views (over the top of Carey's neighborhood) and because of this, would be prized. However, Carey's neighborhood, without the natural hillsides, would lose its greatest attribute and values would stagnate, or go down.

The developer checked through the land titles and discovered that the hillsides had never been deeded to the city. Rather, the original owner, a bank, still owned them. He contracted to purchase the land from the bank. All that he needed now was a waiver from the master plan.

The developer realized he was going to have a battle on his hands. The property had already been designated as open space. To make the deal work, he had to get the local planning commission to set aside the master plan in that area.

He found just the wedge to help make this happen. He intended to show that the overall community needed new housing and there simply wasn't any developable space left. The hillsides were perfect, and since they had never been deeded to the city, giving him the waiver would serve the community interest. He spent money to create an environmental impact report to support his proposal. Then he went before the planning commission.

However, he was sneaky about it. Everything has to be on the planning commission agenda. However, he feared a backlash from Carey's area if the neighbors found out. His plan was simply listed as an enhancement of the existing master plan. The hills in question weren't specifically in the title, although they were the subject of his environmental study. Thus, no notice was given to property owners in Carey's neighborhood. The developer hoped to get things passed without opposition.

Carey and her neighbors might have been faced with a "done deal" if one of them hadn't noticed an engineer tromping over the hills, taking pictures, and making notes. When asked, she revealed the environmental study she was helping to generate.

The neighbor told Carey and she contacted the company making the environmental impact report. It was forthright about what was going on. Carey then contacted the planning commission and was told that, yes, a proposal for removing a section of open space was coming before them in a few weeks.

Carey alerted her neighbors to what was happening and they were just as upset about potential loss in property values as she was. She started a petition against the proposed change and gathered over 400 signatures. On the night of the hearing, 27 of her neighbors were there. Since the procedure for speaking was that each person had to fill out a 4 by 5 card in advance, the commission realized there wasn't room in their regular meeting place and moved to the bigger city council chambers. Since each person who filled out a card was given five minutes to speak, Carey's neighbors talked against the proposal for over two hours. The developer only had half an hour to present his proposal.

But his careful environmental study carried weight. Instead of simply knocking down the plan, as Carey had hoped the planning commission would, it held it over for advisement. The developer might still prevail.

However, Carey had alerted the local newspaper to what was happening and a reporter covered the meeting. Local newspapers can't compete on the international, national, or even state level with larger media. Instead, they like to feature events of local importance. It helps sell their papers. So Carey and her "protesters" were on the front page the next day. Suddenly the entire community was aroused and fearful that what happened to Carey's neighborhood could happen elsewhere. They quickly took up her cause.

With pressure mounting, the city council members at their next meeting listed the proposal on their agenda, listened to dozens of residents, as well as the developer, and then voted 7 to 0 to direct the planning commission to turn down the development, which it immediately did.

Can You Really Do It?

I've condensed what happened to make it more readable. It actually took over a year and a half for Carey's group to succeed. Nevertheless, if Carey prevailed, why can't you?

$$$$$

Work on the School Board.

The single most important influence on a neighborhood's home values is the quality of its schools. When you think about it, this makes sense. People want their children to attend the very best schools. Since the vast majority of people send their children to public schools, they will pick neighborhoods based on how good the schools are.

Your neighborhood may be wonderful to look at, may have pleasant parks and wide streets, may have great access to transportation, and be close to shopping. But, if the schools are bad, you won't see the rapid price appreciation found in areas with good schools. Indeed, depending on just how bad your schools are, you could see prices stagnate or even go down.

It is important for every homeowner to take the time to learn about local schools and to do whatever is possible to improve them.

Note: Better schools cost more. Hence, in neighborhoods with good schools, there will tend to be constant bond measures put before the public to raise money for the schools. However, many property owners vote against these bond measures mistakenly believing that the increased taxes will scare potential buyers away. It just doesn't work like that. Most buyers will gladly pay a few extra tax dollars a year to live in an area with great schools. In fact, they consider it the price they have to pay to get quality schools. Just see what happens if you tell a buyer that the local schools are terrible, but who cares because your taxes are a couple of hundred dollars a year less!

What Can You Do?

A wise homeowner can enhance the value of his or her property with regard to local schools in several ways. These include:

1. *Check out test scores.* Today almost all school districts have their students take standardized tests and the scores are readily available to the public at the district office. (Not the individual student scores, but how the schools and the district as a whole did.) Use good scores to promote the sale of your home. Use bad scores as a wake-up call to get something done to help your neighborhood schools.
2. *Learn about your schools.* Attend a few Board meetings. Find out what the issues are. Support those issues that will make the schools better, work against those that will weaken the schools.
3. *Promote school bond issues.* Yes, I realize this flies in the face of what many people believe. It's especially irksome for those whose children have grown up and left home. Why should you pay for schools that you don't use? On the other hand, you want your property values to go up, don't you? And the surest way of seeing that they do, over the long haul, is through having better schools. Don't spite your face by cutting off your nose . . . work for school bond issues.
4. *Clean up school sites.* All school districts are short of money these days. In most areas, something like 75 percent

or more of school funds go to pay teacher salaries. That leaves very little available for the "plant" itself. As a result, many school sites are rundown. There are weeds in the yards, the fields aren't mowed, classrooms aren't painted; in some extreme cases, the bathrooms don't have toilet seats or toilet paper. A setting such as this is not conducive to learning, morale, or even safety. Organize your neighborhood to give direct help in these needed areas.

Getting Started

You can attend a couple of Board meetings, check on standardized test scores, promote important issues, and support bond measures. In addition, the one area where you can make a big difference overnight is in cleaning up the school site.

Rita was a young mother whose children attended Sequoia Elementary School. She lived in a modest, but nice neighborhood. She and her husband planned to stay there a few years until their income increased to the point where they could move up to an even nicer area. Rita was determined that no matter what, she was going to get the most profit from her home.

Years before she planned to sell, she talked with neighbors who had their homes up for sale. They complained about having trouble getting their prices and finding buyers. They said that potential buyers would drive by the local school, see what terrible condition it was in, and look elsewhere, even though the test scores were not all that bad.

Rita decided something had to be done. So she went to a School Board meeting and during the part where the public was encouraged to ask questions, demanded to know why the Board didn't clean up Sequoia Elementary?

The superintendent gave an answer as did several Board members, all of which came to the same thing: They would try, but there simply wasn't enough money.

Rita asked if she and her neighbors could help clean up the school on a few weekends. The superintendent and the Board conferred and said it was a great idea, provided she submitted plans in advance for what was intended. They didn't want the school painted purple!

Rita knew many other families because their kids all played together. She called meetings, signed people up, and raised a few hundred dollars. Throughout she hammered home two themes that everyone could relate to: A better school meant a better education for their children and a better school meant higher property values.

On a selected Saturday, the families turned out. They weeded around the school and planted flowers and even put in seed for some additional lawn. They also began painting the outside of the building. This was a project that took four separate weekends. By the fourth weekend, there were more neighbors participating than at the first! They had a barbecue going to feed the workers, and there were soft drinks and games for the children. It became a neighborhood picnic that no one wanted to miss. The crowning achievement was when a local artist painted the name of the school across the front in bold letters.

Of course, Rome wasn't built in a day and just painting the exterior wasn't all that was required. Over the next year, teams of neighbors, with the aid of teachers, painted most of the classrooms, fixed and cleaned up the bathrooms, and even paid for an awning to go over the area where the children sat outside to eat their lunches.

The school never looked better. The parents went to the School Board and demanded it be maintained and the Board found the money for a regular maintenance person to keep the lawns mowed, the weeds pulled, and the bathrooms clean.

The result was that the school became an asset to the community instead of a liability. When real estate agents drove prospective buyers to see homes for sale, they made a point of driving by the school, instead of avoiding it. Indeed, the school became the focus for neighborhood meetings and a strong neighborhood NAC emerged.

Best of all, test scores in the school began to rise. Suddenly, everyone was proud to be going to Sequoia Elementary School and it showed in all sorts of ways.

Think it can't or won't happen? Think again. Academic studies repeatedly show that the school environment plays a big role in academic success. Put children in a better environment and they do better.

Similarly, better schools mean a better neighborhood and more people want to live there, thus increasing housing prices.

Note: In some communities, busing is a common practice. Even with busing, improving local schools still should improve local housing prices.

TECHNIQUE **19**   **$$$**

Contact your public works department.

We all pay a lot for public services, however, we don't always get what we pay for. Frequently the money goes to a few neighborhoods at the expense of others. That could mean that your roads desperately need repaving, the sidewalks are broken and weed strewn, the street lighting is inadequate or does not work properly, the streets themselves are seldom cleaned, and on and on.

If this description fits your neighborhood, then you can be assured that the problem is going to adversely affect your property's value, if it hasn't already. Conversely, by remedying the problem, you can often quickly increase the value of your neighborhood and your home.

Consider what a buyer sees when driving up to purchase your home (or your neighbor's). If the streets and sidewalks are well kept, the area looks neat and tended. If there are big cracks in the road with lots of potholes, it looks like the area is decaying and on the way down. If you were a buyer, would you even bother to look at the home if the streets and sidewalks looked bad?

Every community has a public works department, although it goes by a variety of names from "streets and sanitation" to "roads and parks." Find out what the department is called and contact them. Explain that they've been overlooking your neighborhood and describe the problem.

Chances are that no one from your area has bothered to call. In fact, this may be the first they will have heard about it. No, don't expect them to run right out to make a correction. But, be sure that at the least your area is put on the list for public works.

What to Do

1. *Assess the problem.* Is it just in front of your house or is the entire neighborhood affected. If it's a localized problem just affecting your property, you're more likely to get quick action, simply because it will cost less to fix the problem.

2. *Determine if there's a safety issue.* If you can demonstrate that safety is involved, your project can jump to the head of their list. If the sidewalk is broken and someone is likely to trip, fall, and be injured, the city could get sued. If a big pothole in the street causes a car to swerve out of control and hit a pedestrian, the city could be liable. Look for safety issues. They make your project a priority.

3. *Determine what needs to be done.* Repaving streets can cost as much as a million dollars a mile. Digging up and putting in new sidewalks can also be phenomenally expensive. Installing street lamps where none before existed is also a serious money project. Don't expect the local government to willingly pay for these improvements. On the other hand, filling potholes and putting on a new coat of asphalt and gravel is relatively inexpensive. Fixing a broken section of sidewalk or repairing an existing street lamp is similarly much more doable. Try to find a fix that's going to be practical in times of tight money.

4. *Contact your public works department.* If you know exactly where the problem is, what it is, and have a suggestion for a possible remedy, you're much more likely to get a fix. Show up with your plans for fixing the potholes and

resurfacing three bad streets in your neighborhood. If you can present a compelling safety reason, all the better.

5. *Go before the commission.* Often there will be a committee or commission that doles out the public works projects. You may need to appear before them to present your case. If you do, be sure you organize your neighbors and appear in force. Remember, nothing speaks louder than an angry group of voters.

What's Likely to Get Done

Once I complained to a streets department that the sidewalk in front of my house was uneven. Some parts were offset by as much as an inch. People walking on the sidewalks could easily trip and fall. It was definitely a safety concern.

Within a month, the department had a crew out there which broke up and removed the old sidewalk and then poured a new one. It looked great and I felt terrific, until a few months later when I received a bill for $1,100. When I called I learned that the sidewalk was technically on my property, although maintained by the city. Fixing it was legally my financial responsibility.

The moral here is look before you leap. When calling to complain about a problem, ask how and who will pay for the repair. If it's you, ask about alternate public funding or bonds, which may be available. At the least, it could stretch your payment out over a period of years. At the best, someone else might pay for it.

Jerry had a problem with a deteriorating street. After the winter storms, ice had gotten into the cracks in the street and the subzero temperatures had caused the ice to expand. Trucks and busses going over the cracks had knocked out whole chunks creating potholes. They were both an eyesore and a safety nuisance. So Jerry complained to the public works department.

Within a week, a crew was out there putting temporary patches on the potholes. These lasted a month or so until the street traffic began breaking them up. What was needed was a permanent repair. But when Jerry went back to the public works department, he was told there wasn't money enough for repaving the streets in his area any time soon. His street was put "on the list," but it would probably be 20 years or more before the city got around to doing the work.

Not good enough by a long shot, Jerry lamented. So he did what it takes. He organized his neighbors who were equally upset about the condition of local roads. They presented a petition and went before the works commission. They took photos that they had blown up to 5 feet by 6 feet. They got the local newspaper there.

When the commission took their case under advisement, they organized protests outside city hall. That guaranteed them front-page coverage in the local paper.

Eventually, they were notified that their streets were placed near the top of the priority list and within the year they were fully repaved.

True, moving to the top of the list meant another neighborhood was moved closer to the bottom. But, it's up to you to take action to get roads, streets, lights, and so on in your neighborhood improved.

TECHNIQUE **20**   **$$**

Go see the parks and recreation department.

It's hard to imagine having something nicer in a neighborhood than a park. It's a place to take walks and appreciate the beauty of nature. Children can use it for playing individually and in organized sports (such as baseball, soccer, and basketball). Indeed, a park suggests an upscale neighborhood, one where anyone would be delighted to live.

On the other hand, what if your neighborhood has a park that's not maintained? Instead of lawns, there are fields of tall, wild grass. Instead of a baseball diamond and stands, there are broken bleachers and a field cluttered with debris? What if the public toilets have become a hangout for drug dealers? Now this park suddenly becomes a real liability instead of an asset. (Indeed, it can be better to have no park at all!) Worst of all, instead of enhancing your property's value, it drags it down.

Putting public pressure on the parks and recreation department can help clean up and maintain any neighborhood park that you have. But, as with schools, be prepared to put out extra efforts yourself.

What to Do

1. *Check it out.* Is your neighborhood park a mess? Does it need major rehabilitation? Or does it simply need a little bit of extra care.
2. *Ask the parks and recreation department to take care of it.* It may be that a phone call or a visit is all that's needed to get action.

— 89 —

3. *Be prepared to do the work yourself.* If you get stone-walled, then it may be up to you to initiate a correction.

Taking Action

Marianne lived in an upscale neighborhood and loved to take walks in the local park. However, the park had a public toilet and it was common knowledge that drug deals took place in it. It was a typical public facility with a single entrance and many stalls inside. It was an ideal setting for illicit dealing to go on inside. As a result, there were cars frequently parked nearby and tough-looking individuals hanging out. It was the sort of thing that gave a good neighborhood a bad reputation and adversely affected property values.

Marianne complained to the parks and recreation department, but was told there was little they could do. They sent a crew down on a regular basis to clean the facility, but short of locking it up, there wasn't much they could do to prevent undesirable people from using it.

Marianne thought surely they could do more. So, she went on to the Internet and explored similar problems. She discovered that problems with public toilet facilities in park areas were fairly widespread and a fair amount of research had been done to determine how to remedy these problems. It had been discovered that enclosed toilets (such as the one her park) were a breeding ground for illicit activities of many kinds, especially drug dealing. On the other hand, a new design for toilet facilities having individual cubicles, each of which opened directly to the outside, had great success in reducing such problems.

She brought her research to the parks and recreation department and was listened to intently. It was news to them, and they created a study group. It took almost six months, but one day the toilet facilities at Marianne's park were remodeled. Just having the facilities closed for a month while work was in progress forced dealers to move their activities. Having the newly designed toilets kept them from coming back.

Additionally, Marianne contacted the local police department and with their help, she and a few neighbors formed a neighborhood watch program. Signs to that effect were posted and whenever something suspicious was going on, Marianne or her neighbors reported it to the authorities, who sent the police to check on it.

Very quickly the area got cleaned up and stayed that way.

Pet Problems

I have a friend in another neighborhood who had a much milder problem, but one that is illustrative of how to get things done.

Ellen liked to walk in the small park near her home. But, so did her neighbors who took their pets for walks. Unfortunately, many of these pet owners did not clean up after their animals. The result was a real mess that made enjoying the park difficult.

Although this is not a problem that by itself is likely to seriously affect property prices, sometimes it's a combination of small things that have a big effect.

Ellen complained to the parks and recreation department, which put up a couple of signs asking owners to clean up after their pets. However, few pet owners paid much attention.

When Ellen went to the department again, she was told that to be really effective, it was necessary to put up a couple of stations at the entrances to the park that would dispense plastic bags that owners could use to clean up after their pets. They could dispose of these in a nearby garbage can.

The problem was that it took someone to check on the dispensing stations every day or so to be sure they were full of the plastic bags. The parks and recreation department simply didn't have the staff to do this. So Ellen volunteered.

Every day when she took her walk, she would take a box of the plastic bags. If the dispensing stations were low, she would fill them up. And it worked! Pet owners took heed and the park was once again a clean place to walk.

Interestingly, this had a snowballing effect. Other neighbors seeing Ellen's action, began taking action themselves. Those near the park trimmed their hedges and bushes and kept their lawns mowed. In short, the entire neighborhood spontaneously seemed to improve. Sometimes, all it takes is one person to lead the way.

Speed Bumps

Allen wanted to get people to slow down by his park. He lived across the street from it and visitors, often kids from the local high school, would come tearing out of its parking lot and race down the street. There were rubber marks on the asphalt where cars had peeled out and the street was rapidly becoming known as a kind of racing strip—not the sort of thing to encourage home buyers.

Allen contacted the parks and recreation department about putting in a few speed bumps to slow down people coming out of the park. At first, he was told that there was a liability problem: Someone might lose control of their car on the bump and this could cause an accident, for which the city might be held liable. The only way to justify the speed bumps was if it could be shown that they were necessary to slow down speeding cars that presented an even greater hazard.

So Allen spent a few weeks counting cars. Using a radar gun borrowed from the city, he tracked the speed of cars coming out of the parking lot. He learned that the average speed was over 50 miles an hour, on a residential street!

When he brought his results back to the parks and recreation department, they were quite surprised and decided to do their own study, which confirmed Allen's findings.

It took nearly six months and had to go through the legal department as well as public works. But eventually, the speed bumps were installed, and the problem was solved.

Allen felt that this improved the quality of life in his neighborhood substantially, and particularly in front of his own house.

Note: Speed bumps can be a detraction! Some buyers dislike having to slow down for them and will avoid neighborhoods where they exist. They can be a double-edged sword.

Techniques for Making a Grand Entrance

$$

Redo your driveway.

After the general appearance of the front of the home and the front lawn, what prospective buyers tend to see next is the driveway. Sometimes, it's the first thing they walk on. Driveways are a critical component of curb appeal; therefore, they are vital to getting top dollar for your home. Improving the driveway can add value to your property.

The problem is that driveways tend to be expensive to redo. Putting in a new asphalt driveway can easily cost thousands of dollars. Change that to cement and you add a few thousand dollars more. Add bricks or decorative cement and the price continues to go up. After a while you have to begin to wonder if it's really worth the investment.

The answer to that depends on what your driveway looks like before the makeover. Have you ever driven by homes and remarked on the beautiful driveway leading to the house? Sometimes it's all bricks, whether individual or stamped concrete. Other times it's tile. Some driveways are stone or rock imbedded in concrete. There are dozens of different driveway materials. The only sure bet is that the fancier the driveway, the better a potential buyer's impression of a home is going to be.

Of course, it's possible to overdo it. I would never suggest an expensive driveway for a simple tract home. It would be out of sync with the house. The quality of the driveway should match, or just slightly exceed, the quality of the home. For a basic home, a clean, neat asphalt driveway is fine. For some mountain homes with long driveways, even gravel will do (especially when the alternative is mud!).

On the other hand, I'm sure you've driven by homes where the driveway was in bad shape. Perhaps it was cement and there were deep cracks in it. Nothing makes a home look more distressed than a cracked cement driveway, especially if it's also stained.

I'm sure you've seen asphalt driveways were tree roots have created bulges, where there are potholes and where there are rust and oil stains. This does *not* say a quality home.

If the driveway looks bad, it's a negative comment on the home. At the very least, a potential buyer is adding up in his or her mind how much it will cost to put in a new driveway. (And buyers *always* figure high.) At the worst, the potential buyer will simply not consider the property. At any case, it means a lower value for you. Improve that driveway and your home's value will go up.

How Do I Do a Driveway Makeover?

1. *Determine what quality is needed.* If you have a mansion, a long stone driveway can be very elegant. Plan on spending many thousands of dollars. On the other hand, if you have a modest tract home, perhaps simply new tar and a gravel covering on the driveway will be enough to spruce it up. Plan on spending around a thousand dollars.

———

Note: Beware of companies and individuals who for a few hundred dollars will "coat" your driveway. Often this is nothing more than thick black paint. It may not even look good immediately after it's done. But after only a season or two, your driveway will look terrible. Painting should never be considered for a cement driveway.

———

2. *See what your neighbors have.* If every other driveway on the street is asphalt, you'd probably be wasting your money on cement (which is more expensive). On the other hand, if every other driveway is cement, you'd be lowering the value of your home by putting in asphalt.

3. *Be creative.* If you have a cement driveway with cracks, see if you can have the cracked areas removed and replaced with wood, bricks, or even new concrete leaving the other uncracked areas untouched. If done in an artistic fashion, it can look great and cost half as much as putting in a new full cement driveway.

4. *Will cleaning do the trick?* Sometimes a driveway is basically sound, however, over time stains—oil, grease, and rust marks—have marred the surface. This can make the driveway look terrible. You may be able to get by with chemical removers—check at an auto supply or building supply store. However, if the stains have seeped below the surface, often the only thing that will get them out is sand blasting. Although it is expensive, it can cost a fraction of what putting in a new driveway will cost.

5. *Consider expanding or contracting the driveway.* Sometimes the original driveway that the contractors put down

is inadequate. They may have been saving money by doing a minimal job. Perhaps what your home really needs is a wider driveway, or a circular driveway around some trees, or even a shorter or narrower driveway to enhance a small house. Paying an architect a hundred dollars or so to give you a few ideas can be money well spent.

When Should I Do the Work?

You should do it *before* you put your home up for sale. Since it's going to take some time to get done, it's probably a good idea to start three months early.

However, having said that, there's another consideration—how does the appearance of your driveway affect the overall look of your neighborhood? In the previous section, we talked about how "bad" neighbors could lower property values across an area. You have to ask yourself if your driveway is contributing to lowering values. In other words, are you actually one of those "bad" neighbors.

The tendency for most of us is to say, to heck with what my neighbor thinks of my driveway. I'll make it over when I'm ready.

Well said . . . but not well thought out.

Property values don't increase overnight. They go up slowly. If your ugly driveway is holding values down for your neighbors, that will come back to haunt you when it's time for you to sell. Remember, you can only get market price for your home and market price is what comparable homes have recently sold for. That means, what your neighbors' homes sold for. If their prices were held down by the appearance of your property, it will eventually hold down your price as well.

It's something to consider.

$

Mend your fences.

Fences have many functions: They help preserve our privacy. They help us determine property boundaries. They keep us from looking directly into our neighbor's yard. They give our home the feel of an "estate," and so on.

Given all the positives of fences, you would think they are a necessity when owning a home. However, that's not the case. In many parts of the country, lots are unfenced. There is no strong divider between my place and my neighbor's. As a result, there's a much bigger sense of open space, and an atmosphere of everyone living in a village. Fences, unfortunately, can isolate us.

As you can see, fences are a two-edged sword. They can be beneficial as well as disadvantageous. One thing is certain, however, if you live in a neighborhood with fences, you must maintain the ones you have. Letting a fence fall into disrepair makes the property look shoddy, distressed. Just repairing a fence and repainting or restaining it can add to the value of your home.

A Fence Counts

I once bought a home in a fashionable area of the East Bay near San Francisco and got a terrific reduction in price because of a bad fence.

In that area, wooden fences six feet high were the norm. This particular property had been fenced on the side and back years earlier and the fence was in a terrible state. There were gaps in it and whole sections leaned precariously to one side or the other.

However, worst of all was that the backyard of this property was in a kind of hole. The land sloped up behind it and on both sides. Thus, the neighbors all around, if they chose, could easily look into this home's backyard. As a result, the property languished on the market without buyers and the desperate sellers kept giving price reductions. They painted the house and fixed the front yard, but apparently, they never suspected that the real problem was that hole of a backyard. It was great for me because I was able to buy the property for about 15 percent below market, which in the hot selling frenzy of those days was a real bargain. That meant that the bad fence situation cost the sellers 15 percent of the potential price they should have realized from the sale.

As soon as I took possession, I planted a wall of some fast-growing trees on the side of the property that was the worst in terms of the neighbors being able to look over. Then I planted some fruit trees in the back of the lot effectively hiding that side. And I immediately contacted the neighbors on the remaining side and arranged for a new fence to be put up splitting the cost with them. (It turned out that the neighbors were just as upset with the dilapidated fence as I was.)

It took three years for those fast-growing trees to grow up and out, but eventually they were nearly 12 feet tall and completely blocked the worst side. By that time, the fruit trees in back had grown to the point where they hid the back neighbor's yard from view. And there was a new and private fence on the remaining side. Yes, the house was still in a hole. But, that hole now looked like a private garden.

When I sold the property, the backyard was no longer a liability, but an asset. I increased the value of the home substantially, just by paying attention to the fences.

Note: On the side where I put up the living fence of trees, I received no complaints from my neighbors. They were just as happy not to be looking into my yard and to have a more privacy. However, in tracts where there is a height restriction on fences, a living wall rising above that height can be considered just as much a violation as any other kind of fence. You could be forced by a neighbor or a homeowners' association to cut it down. Since I'm sure you don't want to get involved in a legal dispute over a fence/boundary (typically the nastiest kind), take time to check your homeowners' associations rules and bylaws.

How Fancy a Fence Do I Need?

If you already have a fence in place, you should consider replacing it with one of like kind, for example, wood for wood, stone for stone, cement block for cement block, and so on. There may even be a deed restriction on your property requiring a certain type of fence.

Don't get carried away with the fence. It needs to look good, but not elegant. If all the homes in the neighborhood have cement block fences, then that's what you should replace yours with. Putting up wood could cheapen your home. Putting in rocks could be overbuilding for the area.

Note: Don't assume that the existing fence is on the property line. It might be; or it might not be. Get a survey to determine where the correct boundary is. Then, if it's entirely your fence, place it a few inches inside your side. That way, you won't be put in a situation with a neighbor complaining. If it's a "neighbor" fence with each of you paying for half of it, you'll probably want to put it right on the boundary line.

What If There's No Fence There Now?

That can turn into a volatile situation. It may turn out that one of the main reasons your neighbors like their homes is because of all the open space around them. If you fence your yard, it may turn out that the open space they like was on your property. When you fence it in, it could turn very nasty with neighbors even going so far as to threaten lawsuits.

My suggestion is that you first be sure of where your boundaries are by getting a good survey. Then, check to see if fences are permitted in your area. Check with any homeowners' association. Finally, proceed only if everything checks out.

Some people advocate letting your neighbors know in advance. Others say to just do it. It really depends on your disposition and what kind of neighbors you have.

Note: If you haven't fenced an area and your neighbors and others have used it as a walkway for years, they may claim prescriptive rights to it. They may claim an easement was created. You may have difficulty in court defending your rights to put up a fence.

$$$

Make over the front of your home.

Makeovers have become common with homes. People these days are always making over their kitchen and bathrooms, and we'll have more to say about that in later techniques. But here, we're going to consider making over the front of your home.

What's wrong with your home's front?

If you're in doubt, reread the first techniques in this book. There we talk about the impact front lawn, driveway, and entrance can make on a buyer who drives up to your house. Remember, *curb appeal* is critical.

Now, we're going to consider another aspect of first impressions, the overall look of the front of your home. We're not paying attention to particulars such as driveway or lawn or front entrance. Rather, we're concerned with the look of the house itself.

Perhaps a few illustrations will help. Some homes have a particular architectural style. They could offer a Cape Cod look, or Southern Plantation, or Spanish, or Midwestern barn, or whatever. One style is no better than another. What kind of style does your home have?

If you answer that it is, for example, California Ranch, then ask yourself, "How well does it fulfill that style?" Does the house have vertical wood paneling, low brick or stone work, a covered front patio, and so on? Or is it just a suggestion of this style? Is there more you can do to make it look better within its style?

Perhaps your answer is that your home exhibits no predominant style. Many homes built over the last few years are like this.

Now, ask yourself if you're happy with the style and appearance of your home? This is more than just asking if the paint looks good or if the front door needs to be replaced. Here, I'm asking if your home has character.

Note: Character is good, but out-of-character is bad. No matter what, you don't want your home to look abnormal for the neighborhood. While there are many things you can do to stylize your house, you want to be careful not to go overboard. Creating a Tudor-style cottage in an area of angular modern homes will make your home incongruous. You won't enhance the value of your property by making it unusual for its neighborhood. In fact, you could lower its value.

Bad Makeovers

I was recently in an area of Los Angeles near the Wilshire district and happened on a neighborhood of lovely Spanish-style homes built around 50 years ago. The homes had covered porch entries with stonework and marvelous wooden frame windows. Though the streets were narrow and the sidewalks bumpy (from tree roots lifting them up), the area had a charm that could not be missed. Its style clearly enhanced values.

Many of the owners had worked within that style, replacing rotted wood, putting on new wooden shingles (a real problem in the land of wildfires), and replacing worn porch floorboards. In fact, many of the homes had been modernized inside, yet restored to their original style outside . . . except for one.

One home had recently been remodeled. All of the façades and stonework had been removed. The house now was a simple rectangular box. An inexpensive asphalt shingle roof had been put on and metal siding finished off the home. All of the original Spanish look had been removed. I can only describe its current style as . . . industrial. It looked more like an industrial plant than a home.

Don't get me wrong. The home was clean and well painted. The lawn, driveway, and entrance were in terrific shape. I'm quite sure the owner thinks that he or she has increased the value of the property with the makeover they did. Unfortunately, however, nothing could be further from the truth. The makeover of the home in question had undoubtedly lowered its value. In talking with a neighbor who happened to be outside, I received the comment that the home was now a true eyesore.

Good Makeovers

You can't turn a frog into a prince any more than you can turn a Spanish-style bungalow into a . . . well, a factory. And you shouldn't want to. Except in unusual cases, a makeover means capturing the original style of the home and, in so doing, dramatically increasing the value of the property.

Nowhere is this more clearly seen than in an older city such as San Francisco. Here, many of the homes were built around the turn of the century and were given a Victorian façade—hand-turned dowels gave a lace-like look to corners and elaborate woodwork was the rule.

Today, many owners have spent substantial amounts of time and money to recreate the original Victorian look of the homes. It's expensive, because when the homes were built, wood factories on the East Coast fabricated all the necessary wooden parts and shipped them West—today those factories are gone and all the work has to be done by hand. However, if done right, the owners usually get a significant increase in their property's value.

Indeed, many of the makeovers involve tearing down cheap siding and other fixes done to the properties in the 1960s and 1970s. These contributed to keeping the price down. Some remodelers, in fact, look for old Victorian homes that had bad makeovers, buy them cheaply, do a good job, and resell for a profit. That's probably the best argument that the right kind of a makeover pays.

How Do I Do It?

There are five steps to a good front makeover:

1. *Determine if your home needs it.* You might think that the front of your house looks fine. Or you might feel that it desperately needs a makeover. Either way, get second and third opinions. Talk to experienced real estate agents. Check with local architects. Speak to a homeowners' association, if you have one. Consult with neighbors. You will undoubtedly find that having other eyes look at your property is very helpful in coming up with ideas.
2. *Check to see if there are limitations on what you can do.* Certain homes are in historical preservation areas, which means you may need special permission to make changes and those will need to be approved. The homeowners' association may require that you maintain a certain style to your home. There may also be other community requirements. Check it out before you spend money that will be wasted.

3. *Do the cheapest first.* Sometimes simply removing some old trellises or adding molding around windows is enough, and it can cost virtually nothing. Why spend big dollars when a cheap makeover will do?

4. *Take a hard look at your windows.* Front windows often help style a home. For example, you may be able to add a French window style, if appropriate, by replacing your existing windows with inexpensive retrofits. It can give your home a whole new look.

5. *Spend the dollars for a major makeover.* Sometimes, to paraphrase the poet Robert Frost, the best way around a problem is through it. If your home needs and deserves it, bite the bullet and do the whole job.

How Much Will It Cost?

A simple makeover involving just changing the front accents can cost only a few hundred dollars. Do a major makeover involving structural changes and the sky's the limit. Just remember to only do that which will enhance the appeal of your property and do the least expensive first, and you should come out okay.

TECHNIQUE **24**   **$$**

Add a tile entrance.

Every home should have an interior entrance or hallway, a sepa-
rate entrance to the home itself, a kind of transition area be-
tween the outside and the inside. Today, builders of new homes
are well aware of this. No matter how inexpensive the new
home, it will always have some sort of entrance. Even if it's just
a few feet of separate space set off from the rest of the house, it
says "entrance." Of course, the simplest way to accomplish this
is with the flooring.

While very expensive new homes will have entire entrance
rooms or halls, even the least expensive home can have a few
square feet of entrance area. It's where you can put a rug for
people to wipe their shoes, a coat stand for their coats and um-
brellas, a small vanity for checking their face and hair before
they go out, and so on.

Don't underestimate the importance of the entrance to
your home. It helps define the quality of your property when
people enter. If your entrance exudes richness, buyers will
think of your home as a rich property and be prepared to make
offers accordingly.

On the other hand, if the entrance is shabby, then no matter
how well appointed the rest of the home, "shabby" is what will
be imprinted on the buyer's mind (remember first impressions
are what count). And shabby is the kind of offers you can expect
to receive.

Look Down

As noted, the easiest way to define an entrance is with the flooring. If the rest of the house is carpeted wall-to-wall or has wood flooring, a different type of floor at the entrance will help set it off.

The simplest way to add a rich touch to your entrance is to have tile flooring. It's a rare house that has tile throughout, hence, entrance tile will define a different area.

A word about tile: It's been used in homes at least since the ancient Romans built their villas on the Mediterranean. That gives it a history of over 2,000 years. During that time, tile has always indicated richness. It's no different today.

The choice you have in available tiles is immense. Probably the most popular are the larger tiles (typically 9 inches to 12 inches square and bigger). These are available in ceramic, marble, granite, and even a number of synthetics. In a sense, it almost doesn't matter what type of tile you choose, since they all signal a fine entrance. As a practical matter, however, you want a tile that will compliment the rest of your home. Your choices include:

- *Shiny or flat finish:* Shiny shows better, but when wet it can be slippery. You don't want a buyer tripping and falling!
- *Muted or colorful:* Marble tiles are typically white or black, although they can come in other colors. Granites are often in the grey to black category although there are some magnificent granite tiles that are yellow to brown. Ceramic tiles can be almost any color; some of the imported tiles from Italy are in a magnificent spectrum of colors while those from Mexico often have delicious

browns and reds. You want the tiles to accent your home, but not dominate it. Try to get a color that makes the buyers "ooh and ahh," but not so much as that it makes the rest of the home look dull by comparison.

- *Large or small grout:* The grout lines between the tiles can be filled with a complementary color and sometimes are as important to the overall appearance as the tile itself. Therefore, the tendency is to use wide grout. Wide grout, however, tends to accumulate dirt and look bad over time.

What about My Existing Entrance?

Most homes already have an entrance. It may already have tile. What you need to decide is whether the original builder put in a rich entrance, or whether it needs to be improved. Also, you need to look at how well the entrance has held up over time.

Think of it this way: Are you proud of what potential buyers will see when they first walk through the doors of your home? (Remember, most buyers first look down, if for no other reason than to see where they are stepping.)

Not sure? Call in a real estate agent for a second opinion. Good real estate agents see houses day in and day out and can immediately tell you whether your entrance needs work, or is in good shape. (They can do the same for a lot of the features of your home.)

Should I Install It Myself?

You can get good hands-on instruction on how to install tile at most building supply and hardware stores (some even offer occasional classes on it). There are also excellent books on the subject out there. (Check my book, *Tips & Traps When Renovating Your Home.*) Laying tile is not hard, as long as you don't mind getting dirty and crawling around on your hands and knees a bit.

Most entrances are fairly small. Typically they are rarely more than five or six feet wide by 10 or so feet long. That's only 50 or 60 square feet. If you're interested in learning how to lay tile (for future remodeling work in your kitchen or bath), this is a great place to begin.

On the other hand, because this is the entrance to your home, you want it to look good. Saving money by doing it yourself is a good idea *only* if the final result is good. If you botch it and make it look amateurish (tiles at different angles or levels, uneven grout, crooked lines, etc.), you're worse off than if you hadn't done anything at all.

Only you can judge your ability to do this work yourself. If you've previously done successful home improvement projects, then you have a track record to rely on. If not, then you're taking your chances.

How Much Will It Cost?

That depends mostly on the tile you buy. You can get tiles as cheaply as a dollar a tile (for the one-square-foot sections). Or they can cost $20 each or more. Usually the installation is the same price regardless of the price of the tiles, unless you get tiles that break easily, or tiles such as granite that may require a special application.

For a typical entrance, it probably will cost you a couple of hundred dollars, perhaps $500, almost certainly under a thousand.

What about Other Materials?

We've focused here on tile because of the elegant look it offers. But, you can just as easily use wood, an offsetting carpet, or some synthetic material.

The idea is to have an impressive entrance. It can be well worth its cost in boosting the value of your home.

TECHNIQUE **25**   **$**

Hang a fancy chandelier.

Who cares about chandeliers? We might as well ask who cares about any light fixtures or door handles or any of the other ornamentation ("jewelry") that your home has. By themselves, they are of limited value. But when it comes to dressing up your property, they add value. More important, they make a statement about the quality of your home. A "fancy" chandelier speaks volumes about the class of your property. It tells potential buyers that this is a home to be considered.

Chandeliers are the one area where almost all new homebuilders fall down. Except for upscale properties (and sometimes even in these), entrances often have only the most basic lighting. In very inexpensive homes, this might only be a flush ceiling light. In more costly properties, it can be in the form of a small chandelier, one that doesn't cost much and doesn't look as though it does.

On the other hand, a rich-looking chandelier that greets a buyer upon entering the home (and, of course, you will have it turned on!) can bring comments such as, "Ooh, that's elegant!" The impression should carry through to the rest of your home.

Aren't Chandeliers Expensive?

Yes, they are. You can easily spend $10,000 on one. Get a chandelier made of Italian glass by the artist Chuhulli and the price bumps up to $50,000 and more. Indeed, you can spend almost as much as you can imagine on a chandelier. But, you don't have to.

Lighting stores feature high-quality chandeliers in the $500 to $1,000 price range. These offer decorative metals, porcelain, and glass (sometimes even crystal, but these latter are usually more expensive).

A less expensive way of getting a nice chandelier is to visit flea markets or garage sales and check the small items ads in newspapers. Often when people take out an old chandelier, if it's of good quality, they will want to sell it. Sometimes these can be purchased for a fraction of their original cost, particularly if they are tarnished or if the wiring is broken. Shine up the metal, take it to a small appliance store to have it rewired (or, if you're qualified, rewire it yourself), and for a relatively few dollars you can have an eye-opening light in your entrance hall.

Don't Overdue It

A word of caution: Beauty can quickly change into gaudiness when it comes to chandeliers. Try to avoid huge fixtures or ones that offer loads of shiny brass or hundreds of hanging pieces of glass (crystal). These are as likely to create a bad impression as a good one. You just want a nice fixture hanging from the ceiling in your entrance.

Also, don't get carried away with the cord holding the chandelier. A simple chain with the wire wound through it will usually do. Sometimes, when the ceilings are tall, a thin piece of dark brass pipe will look good. Usually you want whatever's holding the chandelier to fade into the background, otherwise it will detract from the piece.

What about Renting a Chandelier?

This is definitely a bad idea. Very few places actually rent chandeliers. Consequently, some intrepid homeowners may think about buying a very expensive chandelier to hang and then returning it to the store once the home is sold. It's sort of like getting your cake and eating it, too.

As I said, this is a very bad idea. Perhaps more problems in selling a home have arisen over issues involving chandeliers than any other. In some cases, entire deals have been lost, in others, lawsuits have resulted.

Over a chandelier? How can that be?

It has to do with the rules over what constitutes real property and what is personal property . . . and it has to do with the buyer's perceptions.

Most buyers who see lighting fixtures in the home, assume they come with the home. The same holds true for front door handles, stoves, and curtains and drapes.

However, in reality, none of these things *must* come with the home. Unless otherwise designated, if they can be removed without damaging the home and replaced by other similar items, they can be considered the personal property of the seller. They can be thought of as removable ornamentation that does not go with the house.

Yes, you can replace a fancy door handle with a cheap one, you can unplug most countertop stoves and take them with you, you can remove curtains and drapes, and you can take down an expensive chandelier (and return it to the store!).

However, don't expect most buyers to stand for this. They will want whatever they saw when they first toured your home. If they don't get it, rest assured they'll be upset if not downright angry. They may threaten to quash the deal or even to take you to court.

To avoid such dire consequences, smart real estate agents will require an inventory. They will write directly into the purchase agreement that all wall hangings, floor coverings, built-in appliances, and light fixtures are included as part of the real estate. This precludes these items from being considered the personal property of the seller. Take them down and you'll be in trouble.

Hence, you can't easily put up a fancy chandelier and then, before you vacate the house, remove it. Indeed, I always tell sellers that if a chandelier is of particular sentimental value to them, they should remove it *before* they put the home up for sale. Replace it with one you can afford to part with.

What about Dining Room Chandeliers?

While we're speaking primarily about chandeliers in the entrance, everything we've said also applies to chandeliers in the dining room or anywhere else in the home. These items reflect the quality of the property.

Which is to say, as long as you're going to dress up the chandelier in the entrance, why not do the same for the one in the dining room, bedroom, and wherever else you may have one?

A fancy chandelier is a luxury. Buyers like to think they're purchasing luxurious homes.

TECHNIQUE **26**   **$$**

Separate rooms.

It's not just walls that separate rooms. Railings, saloon doors, even curtains can be used to divide a larger area into two distinct, smaller ones. However, just how the division is accomplished speaks to the quality and modernity of the home, and also the price it can command.

For example, a few years ago, it was quite common in many homes to have a wrought iron railing (sometimes with a wood topping) used as a separator. It divided living room from dining room or from family room. The iron railing was typically painted either white or black. In its time, it was considered quite chic.

However, that time has passed. Today, most home buyers are looking for something quite different. Often the division between living areas is far more subtle. It can simply be the transition between carpeting and tile or wood flooring. Sometimes an arch built in as part of the wall will suffice. Other times a large opening in the wall—not a walk-through, but a see-through, is used. In short, almost anything *except* those wrought-iron railings.

Similarly, at one time saloon doors were commonly used to separate dining rooms from kitchens. These are half-height double doors that are spring-loaded to remain closed. They don't reach to the floor or ceiling; they're just at head-height to make it difficult to see into the next room. Originally most were stained dark, but some were painted in light colors.

While saloon doors have again begun appearing in a very limited fashion in some very expensive homes, most people consider them passé and, like wrought-iron railings, they tend to date the home.

Finally, there is the matter of using cloth, beads, or other similar materials as a barrier between rooms. These were typically hung in doorways where opening the door took up too much room. They have become symptomatic of inexpensive homes and suggest the room layout is awkward or simply too small.

What all of these room separators have in common is that they date the property. They make it look old and they detract from its presentation. A quick and usually not too expensive way to improve the value of the property is to remove and replace them with another, more modern type of separator.

Will this add significantly to the value of the home? Yes, but in a subtle way. It can convince the potential buyer that the home is not dated, but is modern, that the buyer won't have to spend a lot of money upgrading the property, and that it's going to take a better offer to make the purchase.

Just Remove the Separators

In some cases, that's really all there is to it. This is particularly the case with those wrought-iron railings. A friend recently bought a home where railings separated the entrance from a step-down living room. The step down was more than sufficient to separate the two rooms. The railing was simply an eyesore that said, "outmoded." So my friend unscrewed the railing from the walls and floor and threw it out.

Unfortunately, that left marks on the walls and holes in the floor where tile was laid. The wall marks were easily patched and repainted, but the holes in the floor tiles were another matter. She could have simply filled them in with grout, but that would have looked like a botched job. Besides, the tile itself was a deep blue color, darkening the room.

So, she paid for new lighter tile in the entrance. The cost was about $700 installed. But, now she has a much brighter entrance. And the separation between it and the living room is modern looking and more spacious. She has enhanced the value of her house, certainly far more than the cost involved.

Removing Door Separators

If you've got beads or cloth hanging between rooms, certainly remove them. With a saloon door, it's a matter of deciding whether it looks ultra-modern or just plain old-fashioned. If you're not sure, take off the doors.

That leaves the problem of dividing the room and, typically, there's not enough space for a regular door. What can you do?

One answer is a pocket door. This is a built-in door that slides into the wall instead of swinging open. It looks good and is designed for small areas. However, it requires that a portion of the wall be removed and then rebuilt to accommodate the pocket. This can cost $500 or more. However, it can dramatically improve the appearance of the home.

What about Banisters?

A word about banisters may be helpful. These are not technically room separators—they are a device to help people climb up and down stairs without falling. Yet, they frequently do separate one area of the room from the other and as such can be prominently seen.

A few decades ago, wrought-iron banisters were the rage. Builders loved them because they were inexpensive to install and home buyers readily accepted them. Today, however, they radiate obsolescence.

Today's home buyer is looking for fine wood in the finish work of a home. In terms of a banister, that means wood dowels and railing. These can be painted. However, when stained a natural color, they add richness to the home and usually bump the value of the property up a notch in the eyes of potential buyers.

Therefore, my suggestion is to remove old iron banisters and replace them with modern wood units.

This can be costly. If you do it yourself, you can buy the pieces at most building supply stores. However, if you have a curved banister, then you may very well need to have it custom designed and built. The do-it-yourself project will typically cost no more than $500 dollars. For a custom designed and installed wood banister, figure on spending $1,000 to $5,000 or more.

It'll be well worth it, however, if the banister and stairway is one of the first things a buyer sees when walking into the home. It can add an element of quality and even allure that could result in compelling the buyer to view your property as more valuable.

Techniques Done with Loving Care

TECHNIQUE **27**   **$$$**

Improve the floors.

When you walk through your home, chances are your eyes glance here and there not really registering on an environment that's totally familiar to you. In fact, most of us rarely "see" our own home. It's become a part of us.

That's not the case with potential buyers. When they first enter a home, as we've noted before, their glances typically move all around the house. They'll look at chandeliers, room separators, wall coverings, the amount and type of furnishings—everything to get an overall sense of the place. Then, almost immediately afterward, they'll look down as they begin walking through your home. They look down to be sure of their footing—to be sure that they don't trip over something unexpected. And in doing so, they make one of their most critical evaluations—your carpeting. (You may have little carpeting and instead have wood or tile floors. We will address that shortly.)

Their evaluation continues as they walk through your home. People spend a lot of time looking down. How your carpeting comes across is a huge factor in their determination of both the quality and the condition of your home—its value.

Great looking carpeting says this is a quality home, worth the price you're asking. Terrible looking carpeting says that they're going to have to spend big bucks to replace it and no-way will they give you your price.

How Can I Improve the Carpeting?

If your home has wall-to-wall carpeting, any real estate agent worth his or her salt will tell every seller to have it thoroughly cleaned before putting the home on the market. A soiled carpet looks terrible and distracts buyers from all the other good features of a home.

However, if your wall-to-wall carpet is more than a year old, cleaning may not be enough. All but the very best quality carpeting begins to show wear within a few months, particularly in heavily trafficked areas. This takes the form of matting, where the carpet seems to lay down heavier in those areas, and discoloration, where the heavily used areas have a subtle change in color tone and texture.

If your existing wall-to-wall carpet isn't spotless, perky, and generally looking great, the real answer is to replace it.

At this point, I'm sure that many readers who have had experience replacing carpeting are shaking their heads. Recarpeting a 2,000-square-foot home can easily cost $10,000 or more. Am I truly suggesting that someone do this in order to improve the value of the home for resale?

Indeed I am. Recarpeting is one of those areas that is expensive, but if done correctly is also where the improvement in the form of a quicker sale and a heftier price can be worth it. Keep in mind, I'm not suggesting this if your existing carpeting is relatively new and in good shape. However, if your carpeting is worn to the point where it detracts from the appearance of your home and, thus, drags down its value, you're far better off getting new carpeting.

New Doesn't Have to Be Expensive

It's a fact that almost any quality of new carpeting will look better, at least for six months, than any existing carpeting that's more than a couple of years old. That's what homebuilders know. They frequently will install very inexpensive carpeting knowing full well that, at least in the short haul, it will look great. And if you're contemplating selling soon, the short haul is your biggest concern.

Further, it's almost impossible to really clean carpeting. It's not like you can take it up and put it into the washing machine. Rather, it's a matter of inserting chemicals, steam, or water and extracting dirt. This is a process that is far less than 100 percent efficient. And it sometimes leaves the carpet stiff and ragged looking. Often after only a few cleanings, the carpet will simply look worn out.

Besides, inexpensive carpeting is available in most areas. You can carpet a 2,000 square foot home with nylon carpeting that will look great for $3,000 or less.

Talk to your local carpet dealer about getting rental-grade carpeting. Explain what you're looking for. You may have to check around, but you can be sure someone in your area is selling rental-grade carpeting. This is the sort that apartment house owners use in their units, that builders use in their models. This carpeting, especially when you get good padding underneath, looks terrific. Usually it looks far, far better than any older carpeting you have in your home.

Three or four thousand dollars spent putting in new carpeting just before you sell is a no-brainer. It's the sort of thing that will get your home sold, fast . . . and for more money.

What If I Have Wood Flooring?

Take a hard look at your wood floor. What is its true condition? All wood flooring, no matter the type of wood, even if it's hard oak, will scratch over time. The more wear and tear on it, the worse it will look. If it's been three or more years since the wood flooring was last finished, chances are it's due for a new refinishing.

Refinishing wood floors, when done correctly, means sanding off the old finish along with a thin layer of wood. Then a new layer of sealant and some sort of stain or synthetic finish is applied.

The downside is that all of your furniture usually must be removed (not just temporarily carried to a different room, as can be the case when recarpeting, but stored elsewhere) for a few days, sometimes as long as a week. The process is also messy, with lots of dust. And the odor of the chemicals used can be quite strong and can linger for several weeks.

The result, however, is usually spectacular. Your floors will shine and say, "Buy me!" to any potential buyers. The cost is usually not as much as for new carpeting, depending on the condition of the floor and the type of wood.

Be careful of finishers who say they can do the job chemically. This usually involves stripping (rather than sanding) and then refinishing. Though far cheaper, in my own experience, this simply does not come out nearly as well.

TECHNIQUE **28** $

Add décor lighting.

Do you pay much attention to light switches? Most of us haven't. Yet, when we walk into a brand new home, one of the things that's likely to strike us is the use of "décor" light switches. Instead of the old-fashioned up-and-down flip switch, these have top and bottom pressure plates. Simply press the top to turn on the lights, the bottom to turn them off. There are even dimmers that operate on touch—just press and hold the surface and the light will dim or brighten. Tap the surface to make the light go off and on.

These aren't just oddities or gadgets. Décor lights are pleasant to use and they signal a very modern home. They are now standard in most new homes. In a resale, they indicate a home that has been updated, that isn't suffering from obsolescence.

Obsolescence can mean the loss in value to a property over time caused by it being outdated. It comes about when the features of the old house are superseded by different and advanced features in newer homes. It's what drags the price of your home down when you want to resell.

However, you can reduce the impact of obsolescence by converting the features of your older home to those found in newer ones. One of the cheapest, fastest, and easiest ways to do this is to replace your old flip light switches with modern décor units.

How Do I Do It?

How many light switches do you have in your home? Most homes have 25 or fewer. Since you can buy the new décor switches for around four dollars each or less, that means that for a hundred dollars in materials, you can replace all of the old light switches in your home. (Dimmer switches are far more expensive, costing around $25 apiece.)

Of course, there's the matter of installation. We're talking electricity here and that's not something for the average person to fool around with. (Electrical shocks can be serious and incorrectly installed electrical appliances and devices can cause fires.)

Hiring an electrician to do the job can be expensive, but not too bad if you can find one who is not too busy and who will do this in off-hours. I recently had the work done on a home I own and the cost including materials was only about $375. (It took the electrician less than six hours to do the work.)

You should also investigate to see if your local building department requires a permit. Typically, these permits cost only $25 to $35 and they include an inspection, which helps ensure the work was done right.

Of course, there are the do-it-yourselfers who are willing to tackle almost any job. If you're one of these, be sure that the power to the entire home is *off* before you start. Be very sure you know what you're doing, particularly if you're rewiring complicated three-way switches. Additionally, be very wary if the wiring in your home is aluminum instead of copper. For a time during the 1980s (and even into the present in some areas), aluminum wiring was used to save money. However, aluminum is not as good a conductor of electricity as copper and, hence, the wires have to be thicker. In addition, special connectors are required to ensure that the aluminum wiring does not become loose over time.

There are many books by a variety of companies that will explain how it's done. I do mean to discourage you from doing any electrical work unless you have experience working with electrical appliances, plugs, and sockets and are competent to handle the job.

What about Changing Colors?

Pay special attention to the color of the switch or socket and the cover plates. Décor switches are widely available in white, almond, ivory, and sometimes brown. As long as you're replacing these switches, you may want to change the color. (You may also be repainting—see Technique 31.) Be sure the switch and cover plate match the new color of your home. (Sometimes contrasting the color of the switch with the color of the plate—almond and white, for example—will give a more striking look.)

Should I Change the Wall Plugs

If you're going to change the wall switches, you might want to consider also changing the wall plugs. The difference this can make is also striking. The new décor wall plugs are square, whereas the traditional plugs are round. (We're talking the outside appearance, not where the prongs go in which remains the same.)

It's not absolutely necessary to change the plugs, since many people won't notice them. (They will notice the switches, however, almost guaranteed!) However, if you like things to match, particularly if you're going with a different color switch than you had before, you'll want to do the plugs as well. The cost is typically around a dollar a plug plus installation.

Changing the wall plugs is somewhat harder than changing the switch plates. The wall plugs must all be grounded correctly and sometimes the plug is used as a connector for more than one line on a circuit. (You may have two, three, or more lines coming into the one box that holds the plug.) In older homes, heavier gauge wiring was often used for wall plugs, typically 12 gauge as opposed to the lighter 14 gauge.

The reason I mention this is that the wall plugs come with easy plug-in connections, but most are designed only to accommodate 14-gauge wire. Heavier 12-gauge wire may require a heavier duty plug, which can cost more.

If you have an electrician do it, expect the cost to be slightly more than for the switches. Although, he or she may cut you a special rate if you do both plugs and switches at the same time.

What about Putting a Switch in a New Area?

This seems to come up whenever the matter of updating switches is discussed. There always seems to be one area or another of the home that doesn't have a light switch, yet needs one. It could be to handle an outdoor light. Or perhaps there's a room that needs a three-way switch (so a light can be turned off and on from two separate locations). Or maybe it's to handle a ceiling fan that automatically goes on whenever the light is turned on . . . and you wish it didn't. As long as you're doing new switches, why not do a new switch location?

Don't do it. Put up with the inconvenience while you're living there and let the next buyer worry about it. Chances are any potential buyers coming through will never notice the problem, anyhow. It's the sort of thing that occurs to you after having lived in the house for some time.

The reason is the cost. Simply replacing existing switches is simple. Everything is already there—wiring, hole, electrical box. You're only taking out an old appliance and replacing it with a similar new one.

However, locating a new wall switch (or plug, for that matter) is much more difficult. It requires locating a source of power that can be tapped into. (Building departments do not like you making connections by cutting into existing wiring in the attic—they prefer all such connections be done at accessible boxes.)

Then, once you get the power, there's the matter of snaking the wire from the attic (assuming you have a big enough crawl space to work in) down through the wall to where you've cut a hole to accommodate the new electrical box. (Getting the hole just right with enough room so that you can anchor the wire, once you get it down, is yet another problem.)

Getting through the wall usually means drilling through two top plates (about five inches of wood). Frequently halfway down the wall you'll run into a firebreak (a horizontal piece of wood nailed in place to keep a low fire from rushing up into the attic.)

In short, it's a lot of work and an electrician might charge you as much to do it as to replace all the switches in your house! Since it's not likely to add a dime to the value of your property, unless absolutely necessary, it is best to let it go.

TECHNIQUE **29**   **$$**

Add light.

I once bought a townhouse to live in without first showing it to my wife. To me, it seemed very nice, spacious, with lots of room for an office, which was my biggest priority.

However, when my wife arrived to see it a few days later, she was aghast. The first words out of her mouth were, "It's so dark!"

As with most townhouses, two walls were common to other units. That meant that those walls had no windows. The only windows were at the front and the back of the unit. And as a result, most of the interior was dark.

Of course, there were lamps on tables and floor lamps and when they were all turned on, the unit was fairly light. However, to run them all the time would have cost a great deal. Besides, my wife says she likes "natural light" and this unit didn't have it.

Fortunately, when the seller's disclosures came in there were a few problems with the unit and we gracefully bowed out of the deal—no sale.

While you may not have a townhouse that you're thinking of selling, you probably do have areas of your home that are dark. Most homes have such areas. They are a definite turn-off to buyers. Not only will they keep you from getting a quick sale, but they will also cut down on the amount of money you'll get in offers.

On the other hand, if you lighten up these dark spots, you can very quickly improve the value of your property.

Add Skylights

My wife's big complaint was not that there wasn't enough light. After all, when all the artificial lighting was turned on, it was plenty bright inside. Rather, her complaint was that the light wasn't natural.

One very easy way to bring natural light to the dark area of a room is to add a skylight. Skylights are available in a great variety of styles and sizes. Some are metal (steel or aluminum), others wood, and yet others plastic (PVC) or fiberglass. Some have vents you can open and shades you can close to reduce the light. You can have lighting installed around the periphery of the skylight so that at night, it can still light up the room. There are even tubular units that are no more than about eight inches in diameter that reflect indirect natural light from outside down through the attic and into a room.

One of the big problems about installing skylights in the past was that they tended to leak when there was a downpour. Today's modern units, however, if properly installed, almost never leak.

The cost of having a skylight installed ranges from a low of about $500 to a high of about $5,000 depending on the type you get and the difficulty of installation.

While adding a skylight will definitely enhance the appearance of a room, it's worth noting that it may not be worthwhile or even possible to add a skylight in some homes. For example, if you're on the first floor of a two-story building, forget a skylight. Or if your attic is exceedingly tall, the cost of putting in the box for the skylight could be prohibitive, not to mention the fact that it would look awkward. Or, if you have an older tile roof, the chances of breaking some tiles and ending up having to replace a portion or all of the roof make adding the skylight problematic.

Finally, there's the matter of doing it yourself. Yes, you can. Skylights these days usually come as complete units. You follow directions for cutting the roof and ceiling holes, creating the supports and box, and then simply install it. However, be sure that you do it as directed, or else it could leak. And you *do* need a building permit in almost all areas to put one in.

Add Indirect Lighting

If you have a dark area of the house that you find cannot be helped by a skylight, you may want to consider indirect incandescent lighting.

This usually takes the form of wall sconces (popular back in the 1930s and experiencing a resurgence of popularity today). When installed and turned on, these lights don't shine down or out, but instead up. Thus, the light is reflected off the ceiling and it gives a very natural look.

While it is possible to overdo it by having sconces in every room or having too many in one room, a few sconces in a living room, dining room, or family room or even in an entrance can add a very nice touch, not to mention giving the area more comfortable lighting. (One technique now used in some very upscale homes is to have a sensor located near the door of the room—as you enter, the sconces are automatically turned on. This produces a really nice effect.)

While the wall sconces have a wide spectrum of price (I've bought them for as little as $15 apiece and as much as $300), the real trick is getting them installed. What's required is going into the attic to locate a power source, then drilling holes and threading the wire down the wall to where it can be used and finally figuring out how to hook it up to a control switch. This is all easy when the house is under construction. But when it's a remodeling job, it can be a real pain. Expect to pay an electrician at least $300 to $500 to do the work for a set of sconces.

You could install them yourself. Check into Technique 28 where we discussed installing a new wall switch for problems here. And if you do decide to do it yourself, be sure that all of the house power is *off* before you do any work. Oh yes, be sure to get a permit.

Recessed Lighting

A few years ago, track lighting was the rage. Today, it's recessed lighting. Recessed lighting is now found not only in kitchens, but in bathrooms, living rooms, dining rooms, and even bedrooms. The reason? It tends to look more like natural lighting than conventional ceiling lamps.

Recessed lighting is fairly easy to install, *if* you have attic space. If you don't have attic space, it becomes very difficult to install.

For safe installations, you must use a metal box approved by your local building department. These are installed above the ceiling and often take up a considerable amount of room.

Unlike the wall sconce, however, it's usually fairly easy to hook up recessed lights to a power source in the attic, since there's no drilling down to a wall location required. Also, it's often possible to connect them to an existing wall switch that was used to turn on/off the original ceiling light.

Once again, if you do it yourself, be sure the power is off and also be sure to get a permit.

$$$

Remove popcorn ceilings.

Do you have popcorn on the ceilings of your home? I don't mean the popped kernels of corn. I'm talking about the white bits of cellulose and other fibers that were blown onto ceilings of most homes from about the 1950s through the 1970s and later. They were also referred to as "acoustical" ceilings, although I'm not certain they had any sound-absorbing properties.

Builders used this material largely because it was an inexpensive way of covering wallboard. Instead of first texturing and then painting, as was necessary for walls, the popcorn ceiling could be blown on with no later painting required—a single step. And buyers, at the time, loved them.

However, over the years these popcorn ceilings have gone out of vogue. Today, they seriously date a home. Many buyers who walk into a home and see the ceilings done this way say, "If we buy this home, that's the first thing we'll remove." Then they begin calculating how inconvenient removing the popcorn will be and how much it will cost and they begin thinking about a different house to purchase, one that doesn't have these ceilings.

You get the picture. Popcorn ceilings say obsolescence. They drive the price of the house down. They make selling more difficult. Remove the popcorn and repaint and your house will perk up. Chances are you'll get more for it than the cost of removal, but even if not, you'll almost certainly get a quicker sale.

Is There Any Danger in Removing Popcorn Ceilings?

There can be. During the time that these were used, and particularly prior to 1978 when most builders stopped using it, asbestos was a prime ingredient in the popcorn. That means that the ceiling coverings may contain significant amounts of asbestos material.

Having asbestos in the home, unfortunately, is a serious matter. Asbestos is a known health hazard. According to the Environmental Protection Agency (EPA) long-term exposure can cause at least three serious illnesses: asbestosis, mesothelemia, and lung cancer. Exposure comes primarily from inhaling the tiny asbestos fibers.

However, simply having a ceiling with blown asbestos in it may not constitute a hazard. As long as asbestos is stable (not disturbed), it is not usually considered a hazard. A popcorn ceiling, therefore, may not in and of itself be a problem.

———

Note: Some people who are concerned about their popcorn ceilings have sealed them with shellac and then painted them with an oil-based paint. Generally speaking, encapsulation of asbestos is considered a suitable way of dealing with it, as long as the process does not disturb it.

———

On the other hand, to get a better price, you may not want to simply seal in the popcorn, but to remove it. The problem with popcorn ceilings containing asbestos is that the removal process often disturbs the ceiling and thus releases asbestos fibers into the air.

What Should I Do about Removal?

The first thing you should do is to have your ceilings tested. You can hire an asbestos inspector to come in and have a small portion of the popcorn removed and sent away to a lab for analysis. If it reveals that asbestos is present, you can then hire a corrective action contractor to remove it.

You can find the names of these people by contacting the EPA (www.epa.gov) or by checking in your local phone book. To find out whether your state has a training and certification program for asbestos removal contractors, and for information on the EPA's asbestos programs, call the EPA at 202-554-1404.

Be sure that the person you hire uses approved procedures for asbestos removal. Done improperly, asbestos removal can cause serious problems. (Do not attempt to sweep, blow, or dust asbestos because this usually just sets the fibers spinning in the air.)

Unfortunately, asbestos abatement can cost serious money. It can easily cost upwards of $5,000 or more to have asbestos-laden popcorn ceilings removed. On the other hand, if you're lucky and your popcorn does not contain dangerous levels of asbestos, it usually costs less than $2,000 to have it removed.

Can I Remove a Popcorn Ceiling Myself?

If there is no asbestos hazard, you probably can. But, be aware that it's a strenuous and tricky process. The way it's usually done is to completely shield the walls, ceiling, and any furniture in plastic. Then the entire ceiling is watered to release the popcorn from the wallboard and to make it stick together. Then it is scraped off, trowel by trowel until it's all removed.

Afterward, ceilings typically have to be retaped (because the water has loosened the old taping) and retextured to give them a suitable finish. Finally, they must be repainted.

Given the considerable and nasty nature of the work involved, you may reasonably conclude that it's easier on your patience and better for your back to hire a professional to do it.

Can I Live in the House While the Work's Done?

Anything's possible, but you're probably better off moving to a motel or a friend's or relative's home. The entire process usually takes a week, assuming the weather's dry. That's two days for removal, a day for taping, another for texturing, and another for painting and clean up. Besides, it's so messy you won't want to be around while it's happening.

Also, it's a good idea to remove as much of your furniture as possible. The removers usually do a good job of covering things, but nonetheless, the mess often gets on furniture and it can be difficult to clean it up.

Popcorn ceilings seriously date a house. Given the concern about asbestos, this kind of ceiling often gives buyers some concern about purchasing. Removal is tricky, but it can yield a healthy profit when you sell.

TECHNIQUE **31**   **$$$**

Paint lively.

Unless your home is almost brand new, or you've just recently had it painted, you should seriously consider repainting the entire interior before putting it up for sale. Painting perks up a home and makes it look lively inside. It gives it a fresh, clean appearance that's attractive to home buyers.

But, you may be thinking to yourself, it'll cost a few thousand dollars to paint my house and I won't be putting it on the market for at least a year. Besides, the current paint isn't all that bad.

If your concern is that it will be a while before you sell your home, then consider holding off on painting. However, keep in mind that the typical home needs to be repainted every four to seven years. If it's been that long, even if you plan to keep the house for some time, perhaps it's now time for painting.

As to whether or not the paint looks good, don't ask yourself. Ask someone else. Bring someone in who hasn't gone through your house before (a real estate agent is a perfect candidate) and ask him how the paint looks.

Scratches and marks that you've become blind to, will pop out at him. And he'll notice dirt and color-fading that you've gotten used to. An honest answer may surprise you. It just may convince you to repaint.

A new coat of paint makes your home look, well, new. And newer sells faster . . . and for more.

What about Cleaning the Paint Instead?

Don't do it. Unless you're talking about a very small area and then only in the kitchen or bath where high gloss paints are typically used, don't consider trying to clean the existing paint. It simply can't be done.

If the paint is more than a year old, it has a coating of dirt on it. No, you may not be able to see it. But take a sponge, find a spot that's hidden, say in a closet, and run it across the wall with a good cleaning agent. You'll immediately see the swipe stand out from the rest of the wall. There will be a color difference. Where you swiped is clean, the rest is dirty.

You may conclude from this that your walls need to be cleaned, and indeed they may need to be—before painting. However, unless you plan to go over every inch of wall and ceiling with a cleaner, and probably several times, you won't get an even look. There will always be some areas that are cleaner and some dirtier. In short, trying to clean walls can become a career.

It's so much easier to paint. Clean off very dirty walls, and then paint over them. If you do it yourself, a roller and tray can make simple work of a room. If you hire it out, you can probably get your entire house painted for around $2,000.

By the way, beware of crayon and marks from grease pens. These will tend to come right through new paint. You can paint them a dozen times, and the marks will still show. The solution is to first scrape as much of the grease mark off as possible, and then use a shellac spray over it before painting. This seals the grease and allows the paint to cover and hide it.

What Color Should I Use?

The quick answer is to say just use light colors. White used to be the most popular interior color. Today, many new homes feature a kind of light yellow or mustard color. Most people, if nothing else, find light colors neutral and not objectionable.

However, that's not really an answer. Today, many upscale homes use a variety of harmonious colors including yellows, grays, browns, blues, and many other deep colors that most of us would never consider using. I've seen homes with gray walls and orange ceilings that were incredibly beautiful.

It takes someone with real knowledge of color to be able to say what will and what won't work in a room. Therefore, before beginning to paint, go down to your local paint store and find out if they have a color consultant. Today many paint stores, especially those that carry quality paints such as Benjamin Moore, Dunn Edwards, and others, have color matching services. For a small fee (or sometimes for free, if you agree to buy the paint there), someone with a good sense of color will come out to your home with a color chart and make suggestions. (Alternatively, you can hire a good interior designer to give you similar advice.)

Consider the various options you are shown. Sometimes color schemes that you never dreamt of will turn out looking terrific in your home.

One approach that has become popular (and that my wife used recently in a house we own) is the textured look or "faux" painting. This is accomplished by dipping a sponge in a solution of paint and thinned glaze and then repeatedly applying it onto the wall's surface. The result is a textured multicolor look that can be quite attractive.

Another approach that has been very effective, particularly in children's rooms, is to apply a pattern repeatedly in a band around the top, center, or bottom of a wall. A template is used and it can feature almost any design from flowers to animals. Used sparingly, it can add charm to many rooms.

What about Baths and the Kitchen?

These are special cases. My recommendation in bathrooms is that you use a high luster paint that contains an antifungal agent. This will help keep mold from growing in this naturally damp area.

Be aware, however, that the best antifungal paint is typically oil-based, which means it smells bad and is tough to clean up.

For kitchens, a high gloss paint is usually recommended because, unlike the flat paint used elsewhere in the house, it can be cleaned. Again, an oil-based paint (as opposed to latex) usually works best here.

There's nothing like new paint to freshen a house and help make it look irresistible to a buyer.

TECHNIQUE **32**   **$**

Frame your home in molding.

At the turn of the twentieth century, virtually every new home that was built had elaborate wood molding. It typically framed all of the interior doors and windows. It was used on exterior windows as well. Molding, in fact, was as common as doors and windows. Every home had many hundreds of feet of wood molding built into it. And that molding was not put up in a stingy fashion. Though seldom of hard wood (soft pines were mostly used), it was often three to four inches wide.

Now, compare the stately homes built over a hundred years ago with those built after World War II and up into the 1990s. The vast majority were tract homes, hastily thrown up with little regard for the finishing details (such as wood molding) found in older homes. Sheetrock was used instead of plaster and, hence, there was little need of molding between walls and ceilings. Windows were often steel or aluminum and they were designed to pop right in with the sash forming the borders. Again, no molding was needed.

Indeed, in these postwar homes, there were only two places that molding was commonly found: baseboards, where the walls met the flooring (to cover an uneven match) and around doors, where the molding blended the door frame into the wall. Even here, however, there was no need for fancy or large molding. Typically a flat molding of less than two inches was used. Hence in the "modern" home of the late twentieth century, molding was simply a utilitarian cover, used only when necessary. The homes themselves tended to be stark, unelaborated, and without much interior decoration.

Now consider the latest homes, those built at the very end of the last century and into the twenty-first century. Most new homes are a throwback to the elaborate styles of a hundred years earlier. Many have wooden banisters, wood flooring (instead of wall-to-wall carpeting), and most now again have wood molding.

Today's modern, new home again comes with molding not just around doors and as a baseboard between walls and floors, but also as casings around windows and, occasionally, as a crown or ceiling trim. Some even use a chair rail—molding around walls at roughly the height of a chair back. Today's modern homes use hundreds of feet of molding that is again wider, sometimes three or four inches wide. When it's not painted, it's often expensive hard wood.

In short, molding is in vogue again. Take a look at your house. You can almost tell when it was built by the molding, or lack of it. In fact, if your home lacks molding, it's seriously dated.

One way of enhancing the value of your home, without spending a lot of money, is to add molding. Add it around windows (which you may have replaced with new double-pane plastic models), replace it at the baseboard and around doors, and in some rooms, use it as an accent border as a crown between wall and ceiling. Use wider molding, three-inches wide or more.

Yes, it will make a difference. Buyers coming into the house will be able to differentiate your home from similar models that have not been upgraded. They will prefer your home, meaning a faster sale typically for more money. Frame your house in molding.

How Much Will It Cost?

I recently had a handyman replace and add to the molding throughout the entire house that I own. He also repainted the whole inside. The cost was $2,500, not much more than the painting itself.

Neither painting nor application of molding is brain surgery, however, you do want to be sure that the person doing the work has done it before and is skilled enough to do a good job. Often a good handyman is just the ticket.

Can I Do It Myself?

Of course, you can. However, it does require that you be able to measure accurately and to cut at an angle (usually 45 degrees).

You can buy molding of all sizes, shapes, and lengths at building supply stores. The price also varies dramatically from a few cents a linear foot to a dollar or more. It usually comes in four grades:

1. The lowest grade wood is laminated (finger-jointed), designed for painting to cover the lamination.
2. Medium grade wood comes in solid pieces, but is usually made of inexpensive pine. It will take a variety of stains, but will dent easily and will not take on the rich tones of hard wood.
3. High grade wood is made of hard woods such as oak that stain well and do not dent easily.
4. Plastic molding comes already painted (at least with a first coat), cuts easily, however, requires care in nailing so as not to dent the plastic, which tends to be soft.

Putting the molding on is the most difficult part of the job. If you aren't experienced here, you may want to hire a pro.

If you are going to stain the wood, you should do this *before* having it nailed to the wall (floor or ceiling). It will be almost impossible to stain it after it is up without making a mess of the surrounding walls or ceiling. If you are going to paint the molding, normally this is done *after* you have it nailed up.

One of the quickest ways of modernizing a home is to replace and add molding. It lets everyone, especially buyers, know that your place is in fashion.

Vital Makeover Techniques

TECHNIQUE **33**   **$$$$$**

Make your kitchen over.

If there's one area of the house that the experts agree about when it comes to improving the value of your home, it is the kitchen. Kitchen makeovers are almost a sure bet, provided you do what's necessary for your kitchen, and don't over do it.

A kitchen makeover typically involves doing *all* of the following:

- Repainting the entire kitchen.
- Putting in new flooring.
- Replacing the cabinets.
- Putting in a new countertop.
- Putting in new lighting.
- Replacing all of the appliances.

If you're going to do a complete makeover, the price can be staggering. It can very easily cost $15,000 and many experts suggest a minimum starting figure of $25,000. From there it can spiral upwards in an almost unlimited fashion, depending on what you put in.

That, of course, is the rub. The key to a successful kitchen makeover is to do just enough, and not too much. However, how do you know what the right balance is? (In the next few techniques, we'll go over partial makeovers, but for here we're concerned with the full job.)

Check for Obsolescence

If your home is more than seven years old, chances are that your kitchen is at least partially obsolete.

How can that be? After all, you've got a sink, stove, refrigerator, and dishwasher that work just like the brand new houses. So, how can yours be "old fashioned"?

The answer is that things change and nothing seems to be changing faster than kitchen technology and fashions. Seven or more years ago, almost any dishwasher would do. Today, it should be one of the new energy efficient, super quiet models.

Seven years ago, a sink was a sink. Today, sinks are sectional with raised scrubbing areas, they have special pull out faucets, come with dispensers for boiling as well as filtered water, and are built in a variety of materials including colored porcelain, high-luster stainless steel, and a wide variety of synthetics.

The same holds true for ovens, refrigerators, and kitchen cabinets. The darker woods of the 1970s and 1980s and the lighter woods of the mid-1990s have been replaced by deep rose colors, mahoganies, maples, and other specialty woods. Glass doors, almost never found during the latter half of the twentieth century, are common in kitchen cabinets as are fancy handles.

The biggest change is in countertops. Today's most popular materials include Corian® and granite, as well as surprisingly colorful tiles.

Look around your kitchen. Is it truly up-to-date? If you're not sure, check out the kitchens in some new model homes in your area. Even the not-so-expensive homes will have elaborate kitchens that may make yours look dated by comparison.

What Are Your Neighbors Doing?

None of us live in a vacuum. Almost all of us have comparable houses nearby. Indeed, the most common way of establishing a price for your home when you sell is to get a comparative market analysis (CMA) that compares your home to recent sales of similar homes.

Perhaps the most important single thing you can do before embarking on a kitchen makeover is to talk to your neighbors to see what they've done. Chances are they have a kitchen similar to yours. If a preponderance of them have done full makeovers, you can feel comfortable in doing one yourself. If none of them have, then you might be overbuilding to do the full makeover. Remember, it is as hard to sell the best house on the block as it is to sell the worst house on the block. Ideally, find out what most have spent on their kitchen makeovers and try not to spend more . . . or much less. You don't want to create a "white elephant," a home where you've poured so much money into your kitchen that you can't get it out when you sell. On the other hand, you don't want to do so little that when it's time to sell, buyers knock the price down because of your minimal kitchen.

What Is the Total Value of Your Home Relative to the Makeover?

Take a look at the likely sales price of your home and try to spend no more than 10 percent on a kitchen makeover.

Admittedly, this is a rule-of-thumb. But, it can be helpful. What this means is that if your house is worth $500,000, you can probably spend up to $50,000 on your kitchen and still get all of your money back. Spend more than that and chances are you're overdoing it and will lose money.

If your house is worth $200,000, try not to spend more than about $20,000 to make it a profitable makeover.

Remember, this is *not* a rule written in stone. Every case is different. Those people selling remodeling work will often tell you that you can get more. Real estate agents listing your house for a quick sale will probably tell you you'll get less. I've just found 10 percent to be a good rule of thumb to use.

TECHNIQUE **34**   ***$$$$***

Put down a new kitchen floor and countertop.

In Technique 33, we talked about a total kitchen makeover. Here, we're going to consider a smaller makeover, one that will greatly increase the value of your kitchen, but at a fraction of the cost.

The two areas of the kitchen that receive the most attention are the floor and the countertops. (The sink and stove are also important and we'll cover those shortly.)

Thus, if you can't afford (or it doesn't make financial sense) to do a complete kitchen makeover, a minimal job takes just these two into account. Replace them and your kitchen will look almost like you did a complete makeover.

Take a Hard Look at Your Cabinets First

You can only put in a new countertop if you have cabinets that will support it. I don't mean just in weight, which is a concern especially if you are going to use granite or concrete, but also in terms of appearance. A new countertop with old cabinets hardly makes sense. Therefore, you must decide whether your old cabinets will work.

This is an important decision because new cabinets for a kitchen can easily cost $10,000 and up. Keeping the old ones and refinishing them can be a fraction of that cost.

The biggest concerns with cabinets is how fashionable they look and what their condition is. Many older cabinets look just as good as newer ones. They are often made of good materials, such as oak or ash. However, over time their finish has gotten many dings and scratches and they look tired. If, however, they are not warped, broken, and do not have veneer separations, they may be perfectly useable. For around $2,000, you can have a good painter come in and either stain or paint them. This usually includes filling in any nicks and at least some minimal sanding. (Be sure the stain or paint is oil-based, otherwise it probably will not stick well.)

As an alternative, there are many kitchen renovators who will come in and replace all the doors with new ones and laminate all the cabinet surfaces with a thin veneer of new wood, and then stain it all the same color. If done correctly, this looks just like new. However, the cost is often two-thirds to three-quarters of the price of new cabinets.

Whatever course you take, you should pay special attention to see that your cabinets look good. There's no point in going through the considerable expense of replacing a countertop, if the cabinets it sits on look bad.

The Countertop Counts

The countertop is the first thing that people see when they enter a kitchen (besides the floor, which we'll cover in a moment). A shiny, fashionable countertop speaks volumes for the quality of your kitchen . . . and home.

Countertops come and go in vogue. Those receiving the most attention today are mixed media. Some of the countertop is made of tile, while other parts are made of granite or Corian. For example, many new models for upscale homes will include traditional tile countertops around the periphery of the kitchen with a granite island in the center. The effect is quite dramatic with the tile and granite offsetting each other. Of course, care must be taken to be sure the colors and textures are complimentary.

If you want to make your kitchen look rich in appearance, go with the trend. That's currently mixed media.

Granite countertops are usually made of huge slices of granite, polished, and then trucked to your kitchen. A wide variety of colors are available, as well as a wide range of prices. The more unusual the coloring, the more expensive the granite. When polished, granite has a remarkable luster. It's very hard, making it a good surface for a kitchen. At the turn of the previous century, marble was often used as a counter-top, but it proved to be too soft. Soapstone, also used, had a similar problem. Granite is harder, however, it's porous so it needs to be treated with a sealer every year or so to be sure it doesn't get stained.

The big problem with granite is the cost. It is sold by the inch and an average-sized kitchen can require $7,000 to $15,000 in granite for countertops (including a low splash board).

However, you can get granite tile, typically sold in pieces one-foot square or larger. This can be laid just like conventional tile, yet it gives a shiny granite look. The cost is usually half that of a slab granite counter.

Plastic countertops such as Corian (produced by DuPont) are also popular. These come in a variety of colors. One advantage is that they are poured (in a factory) and the seams are then melded together. Thus, you end up with one solid countertop.

Corian, however, costs almost as much as granite. And it will char if something very hot is laid on the surface. (However, burns can be cut out and replaced almost seamlessly—although not without considerable cost.)

Of course, there's always tile. Used by the ancient Romans, it's always a popular choice. A good tile countertop means an efficient, clean kitchen. These days, tile can be as rich and as expensive as granite. There is glass tile, molded decorative tile, Italian and Mexican tile, and so on. The sky is the limit.

Whatever you choose, a new countertop (along with renovated cabinets) will make your kitchen a plus instead of a minus and should add value to your property.

Change the Flooring

Along with the countertop, you also need to do something with the flooring. If the flooring in your kitchen is more than seven years old, it probably needs to be refinished or replaced.

There are many wood alternatives today in the form of laminated floors that cost a fraction of real wood. (Pergo® is one well-known brand.) Laminated floors consist of a thin layer of compressed wood covered with a laminated hard surface with a "picture" of wood on it. The floor is typically floated, meaning it's not glued down. It's held in place by its edges, which are glued and which butt up to walls or cabinets. It looks just like real wood, except that the feel when walking on it is different. Because it is not glued down, some people say it has a hollow sound when walked on. Also, if it is damaged by having something fall and mar the surface, it usually cannot be repaired except by replacing several boards—a fairly expensive undertaking.

Existing tile floors may need to be regrouted. Today's fashion calls for large tiles in subtle shades of color and texture. You may be better off simply removing an old tile floor and replacing it. Tile floors are not inexpensive, but they are typically not as expensive as wood.

Linoleum (either as a sheet or in squares) can also be used as flooring, but it certainly does not make a statement about the richness of a house the way wood or tile does.

TECHNIQUE **35**   **$$$**

Replace kitchen appliances.

What if you don't want or don't need a major kitchen makeover? What if your countertops look great and the flooring in your kitchen is fine? What if the kitchen cabinets shine? Does that mean that you're set and there's nothing you need to do to enhance your kitchen's appearance?

Before you pat yourself on the back and move on, take a long look at your kitchen appliances. These include:

- Stove/oven/microwave
- Dishwasher
- Sink/garbage disposer
- Compactor
- Refrigerator

Chances are that if your home is more than 7 to 10 years old and you haven't yet replaced any of these items, they're ready to be replaced now. Besides simple obsolescence, there's also wear and tear. Dishwashers rarely last more than 10 years. The inside trays begin to rust, the front door gets scratched, and they begin to leak.

Stoves will sometimes last the lifetime of the home, but their appearance can get ragged with scratches, scuffs, and dull marks, not to mention chips or scratches. If they're electric, the burners will get tarnished and look like they need replacements.

Sinks also get nicked and sometimes stained. However, their biggest problem is obsolescence. Today, most people prefer the offset sink with a small higher side for the garbage disposer and a deep, wide side for soaking. The shape (not to mention the color) of your old sink may be outdated.

Refrigerators, however, are another matter entirely. Since you normally do not leave these with the house, but instead take them with you, it would seem that they should not matter. Yet, refrigerators take up so much space in a home that their very prominence makes them either an asset or a liability. Just adding a new refrigerator can perk up your kitchen. And what's more, unless it's a built-in, you can take it with you when you leave!

Take a good look at your kitchen. Are its appliances holding it back? Are buyers going to look at the kitchen and start adding up the money it will cost to replace those items? (Remember, buyers *always* figure high.)

Are your kitchen appliances telling the buyer to consider your home a fixer-upper?

What Should I Replace Them With?

Any new appliance usually looks better than an existing old one. And they don't have to cost that much. $2,500 to $3,500 spent on upgrading appliances in a kitchen can often result in far more in return when you sell.

Here's what I would consider doing:

- *Kitchen sink:* Replace it with one of the stylish new models offered by leading manufacturers such as Kohler or American. You can choose from colored porcelain or stainless steel. (If you go with stainless, be sure to get a high-quality grade, otherwise water stains will make it look bad.) Dark colored sinks are now the rage, but be sure the color complements the kitchen colors and does not clash with them.

Also, be sure to put in a new faucet. Popular brands such as Moen, Price-Pfister, and others offer stylish designs at reasonable prices. You can use the old garbage disposal, if it works well, but a new one isn't that expensive when you're replacing the sink. The total cost for sink, faucet, and disposal shouldn't be more than $2,000, including $300 to have a handyman or plumber install it.

- *Stove/oven:* If it's a built-in, it will probably be cheaper. The new models include electric glass tops (invisible burners) or high-tech gas with igniters. They have digital controls and look every bit like twenty-first century appliances. You can get a good one for around $700. If you can't install it yourself, usually the store where you buy it will handle delivery and install it for around $100.

- *Dishwasher:* This is where high tech has come into its own. The newest dishwashers, such as those featured by Bosch and Maytag, are whisper quiet. Some have stainless steel drums and are oversized for big loads. Many of them have built-in disposals. Plan on spending $600 for a middle-of-the-road model and another $100 or so to have it installed. A top-of-the-line model can easily cost $2,000 and more.

Note: Many building departments require a permit to replace a dishwasher even if you use a contractor.

- *Compactor:* If you don't have one, consider putting one in. Since buyers know these are typically found only in upscale homes, it will make a statement about your home.

Usually you will have to sacrifice a cupboard to create space for the compactor unit. You'll need to have an electrician put in the correct voltage line for it, if you don't already have one conveniently located.

- *Refrigerator:* This is the biggest expense. If you already have a built-in (such as a SubZero, General Electric, Amana), take a good look at the front. Typically you can replace the front panels for a few hundred dollars to give the refrigerator a new look. Consider doing it.

  If you have a stand-alone, then it's probably not worth the expense of putting in a built-in. Someone would undoubtedly have to tear into your kitchen removing cabinets and perhaps even hacking into walls to make room for it. It is better to simply replace your existing stand-alone refrigerator with a new, modern model.

  There are literally hundreds of models to choose from coming from a dozen different manufacturers. I suggest a double door unit with an ice-maker and water dispenser on the front. But be careful. While it's nice to go for the biggest model you can get, these units take up a lot of room. Their size can dwarf your kitchen. Sometimes it's better to get a smaller model simply because it won't take up so much room in the kitchen and will make the room look more spacious. Just remember, however, that you'll need something you can live with because chances are you'll end up taking it with you.

Replacing your kitchen appliances isn't cheap, but then again, it isn't that expensive, either. For one of the lowest cost kitchen makeovers, it can be the way to go.

TECHNIQUE **36**   **$$$$$**

Do a bathroom restoration.

Most experts agree that second to a kitchen, a bathroom is where you can dramatically improve the value of your home. Of course, it's possible to sink vast amounts of cash into a bathroom and never get it out. However, if done judiciously, a bathroom restoration definitely will enhance your profits when you sell.

A quick word about my use of the word, "restoration." Unlike a kitchen, where modernization is usually the key to success, in a bathroom, often it's returning it to a style that it once may have had (in the case of an older home), or creating a style for it that it may never before have had. Bathrooms are where you can build dreams into a home and where it's almost impossible to be too elaborate.

If you're not sure of what I mean, once again visit some model homes being built nearby. Take a look at the master bath. In today's homes, these bathrooms are often as big as the entire bedroom. They can remind you of a scene from the *Arabian Nights*.

Even in modestly priced homes, there will often be a separate shower stall and tub with recessed and make-up lighting, plus double sinks. Typically there will be tile, Corian, marble, or granite on the countertops. The fixtures may be highly stylized. In short, the master bathroom is where the builder spent a lot of the money. Taking a cue from builders who are experienced in what sells houses, you may want to do this as well.

Buyers love to anticipate using a master bathroom. It's a place of relaxation as well as imagination. That's why it's become common to put a whirlpool tub (such as a Jacuzzi®) in the master bathroom of upscale homes.

What about Size?

In an existing house, the biggest limitation in a bathroom restoration is its size. When building new, it's easy to create a large bathroom (just steal the space from other rooms and closets). With an existing house, you usually only have the original space to work with.

Note: You can always add on to the size of the master bathroom. But, this constitutes major work and the cost immediately skyrockets. Except when the existing bathroom is simply too small for the home, it's not something that will usually return your money from the investment. Enlarging the bathroom is a money pit that is to be avoided, if possible.

What Should I Do?

As with the kitchen, the biggest expense can be the countertop, if you choose to go with granite, marble, or Corian. However, many people expect tile in a bathroom, so it is quite acceptable to use tile for countertops, floors, and even walls (usually up to half way up).

The tiling of a master bathroom can easily cost a few thousand dollars, if you do an extensive job. Getting a stylish colored toilet can add several hundred dollars more. (You can spend thousands on a toilet, if you really want to get elaborate. There are even designs that blow hot and cold air!)

A new shower can be incorporated in the tile work. A whirlpool bath such as a Jacuzzi® can be purchased for as little as $500 or as much as well over a thousand. It usually will require a dedicated electrical line and you'll have the cost of the electrician, not to mention the installation of the tub itself that may require a plumber . . . and we all know how much they charge!

Bathroom sinks run the gamut of costs from simple units that cost as little as $50 to elaborate sinks with fluting, inlaid designs, and even drawings in them that cost thousands. If you're thinking primarily of resale, I would suggest a porcelain (not metal) sink at minimum. You can get a decent one for around $250. Be sure to get a good faucet. These can be found at plumbing supply stores for another $250 or more.

As a rule of thumb, the amount you spend on the bathroom should not be more than 5 percent of the home's value. That means on a $200,000 home, you can probably get away with spending about $10,000. On a $500,000 home that amount moves up $25,000. Either way, you should dramatically improve your home's value.

What about Spending Less?

If you're short of cash and want to maximize your profits, there's always the quick and simple makeover. Here you can do the following:

- *Replace the countertop and flooring with inexpensive tile.* This is not that costly and depending on your tile selection and who you find to do the job, it can be done for around $1,000 for a typical smaller sized bathroom.
- *Replace the sink and faucet.* Add another $300 for both, if done minimally, and another $100 to have it installed.

- *Refinish the tub.* Assuming you're not going to add a new whirlpool tub, consider having the existing porcelain tub refinished. The cost is around $200 and you save the money you would otherwise spend on a new tub, removal of the old (often a frighteningly difficult chore), and purchase of a new one.
- *Redo the shower.* If it's a tub shower, this usually means tiling the walls above the tub. If it's a stand-alone shower, it means retiling the shower itself.
- *Add new towel racks, repaint, and put in new light fixtures.*

The total cost of a quick and simple makeover need only be a few thousand dollars. If done prudently, it will add multiples of that amount of money to the value of your home. However, don't confuse it with the elaborate remodeling required of a full makeover, or the impression that a makeover can create on a home buyer.

TECHNIQUE **37**   **$$**

Relight your home.

Lighting makes a huge difference. As we noted in Techniques 25, 29, and elsewhere, you want to have as much light in your home as possible. It makes your home look bigger, airier, and more desirable to buyers. As discussed in Technique 28, hanging a new chandelier in the entrance and dining room can add significantly to the value of your home.

But that only takes care of the entrance and possibly the dining room. What about the rest of the rooms in your home? Don't they need light as well?

Yes, they do and relighting them can make a big difference. In fact, when talking with sellers who have their homes on the market, I recommend that they purchase half a dozen of those inexpensive halogen lights and put them in each room. Yes, they use a lot of electricity, but the extra light often makes the difference when a buyer is on the fence and can't decide whether or not to make an offer on the home.

However, in your case, if you have the time to relight your home, my suggestion is that you go through each room, including the bedrooms, and replace all of the old fixtures.

This is especially the case where the light fixture is one of those old, inexpensive ceiling models that sell for around $10.

Go down to one of the building supply or specialty lighting stores and purchase some nicer ceiling lights. For around $40 or $50 each, you can get some quite attractive light fixtures. That means for a couple of hundred dollars you can replace all the ceiling lights throughout your home, except the kitchen and bath which we'll discuss next. Be sure the fixtures produce a lot of light, at least 200 to 300 watts total for each.

Now, no matter which room a prospective buyer walks into, it will be lit brightly. And the lighting fixture itself will be modern and attractive.

What about the Kitchen and Bath Lights?

These are special cases. Most designers suggest that you use at least one fluorescent fixture in the bathroom. This saves money and usually gives off lots of light. My suggestion is to have two lighting sources in the bathroom, when possible. Use a fluorescent overhead. Then use make-up or similar lighting near the main mirror. The lights themselves are relatively inexpensive and shouldn't cost more than around $100. However, if you don't already have appropriate wiring, hiring an electrician to install them can add up to a hefty sum and may make you re-think doing it. Maybe one strong ceiling light will do after all!

Older kitchens often have fluorescent lighting. The problem here is that fluorescents give off a green cast. While our brains tend to compensate, nevertheless these lights can give eggs and mayonnaise an unhealthy looking green pallor, not something that's desirable in a kitchen.

My suggestion for the kitchen is recessed lighting. When done correctly, this can be fairly inexpensive and, when using tungsten lights, will give everything in the kitchen a golden glow—much more appealing.

Assuming you have attic space above the kitchen, installing recessed spot lighting is usually quite easy and inexpensive. If you don't know how to do it yourself, hire a handyman or electrician. Typically they will cut appropriate sized holes in the ceiling, attach metal "pots" that hold the lights to the ceiling joists, and connect them to the electrical system and a wall switch. The total cost for a kitchen can be well under $1,000 including materials.

———

Note: A permit is almost always required for all electrical work whether done by you or a professional. Be sure that you get a permit because you'll want to disclose this to a future buyer. Also, be sure the electrical fixtures you use are approved by your building department—not all are! If you decide to do it yourself, always be sure that *all* power is turned off!

———

The only real problem comes in removing existing fluorescent light fixtures in the kitchen. These may be recessed into the ceiling or may hang down. Either way, their removal may leave behind an unsightly gap or hole in the ceiling. You will want to have these taped and textured (or, in an extreme case, have new wallboard installed).

What about Backyard Lighting?

Most homes come with one small light just outside the back door leading to the backyard. This is hardly enough to light up the backyard, particularly if you have it landscaped. Remember, many buyers will probably come back at night for another look at your property. Therefore, relighting the backyard can be considered a necessity.

But, it doesn't have to be expensive. For example, in my current house, wiring leading off the existing backyard light goes to three different locations with spotlights. When I flip the existing wall switch, the entire backyard is illuminated, something that will make any buyer appreciative. I also use low-voltage lighting in the darker areas of the backyard for accent.

If you decide to relight your backyard, unless you're an electrician, be sure to consult with one. The reason is that outdoor lighting must be properly installed and grounded. Many building departments require that any wiring that is exposed (outside of the home's interior walls or attic) be carried in waterproof metal piping. This piping is not expensive, but it is difficult to bend and fit correctly.

Building departments also typically require a ground wire be run within the electrical piping and that a ground fault interrupter (GFI) breaker be used. This is to help ensure that if there should be a fault in the circuit, someone (such as yourself or a buyer!) would not be electrocuted. All of which is to say that if you're not a pro, having a professional do it makes good sense.

Materials for outdoor lighting in the back of your home may be inexpensive, but it could get costly getting the lighting installed. Be sure to get several estimates from licensed electricians. As always, if you do it yourself, be sure *all* power is off!

Relighting your home won't make as much difference as, for example, making over your kitchen or bathroom. Then again, it will only cost a fraction as much. If done prudently, it can help sell your house quicker and for more money.

TECHNIQUE **38** $$$

Add a new bathroom.

Here's a quick way to add $25,000 or more to the value of your home, or lose about $25,000—add a new bathroom.

Adding a bathroom is problematic. Where it's needed, it adds value. Where it's extra dressing on the house, it's a money pit. The big question is how do you decide if adding a bathroom will add value?

This really isn't hard. Ask a real estate agent to get you a comparative market analysis (CMA). Virtually all real estate agents will provide them for free in the hope that when you're ready to sell, you'll list with them.

The CMA is a list of all recent homes sold in the area that are comparable to yours. Usually it's used to help you determine price. But, here we're going to use it to help you determine if it's wise to add another bathroom.

The CMA will almost certainly list the rooms in the homes sold, including the number of bathrooms. Now, compare the number of bathrooms in homes sold to the number in your home.

If all the homes sold have two baths and you have two, you're fine. Adding another bathroom, while it might jazz up your home a bit, will be a waste of money. The reason is that buyers of homes like yours won't be expecting it . . . and they certainly won't pay more. Most of whatever you put into that bathroom will almost certainly not be recouped.

On the other hand, if all the other houses have two bathrooms and you only have one, or if they all have three and you only have two, then by all means consider putting in a new bathroom. To do so will simply bring your home up to the expectations of buyers.

Without that bathroom, they will see your home as having functional obsolescence, and they will cut the amount they offer (if they make offers) by a substantial amount. With that "extra" bathroom (actually, it's not extra—it just brings you up to what similar homes have), you can expect a far higher price.

The rule is simple when it comes to bathrooms. You need to have as many as your neighbors do. Any less will impede your sale and will significantly cut your price. Any more will just be extra icing on the cake and usually won't make back enough to be worthwhile.

What Does It Cost to Add a New Bathroom?

With the exception of completely making over your kitchen, it can be the most significant expense you'll have. It all has to do with dragging hot and cold water pipes and connecting to a waste water (sewer) system.

However, it is possible to do it efficiently and somewhat inexpensively. It all comes down to where you place it.

If your house has only one bathroom, chances are it's in the hallway so it can more easily be accessed from all of the bedrooms. However, most people want at least one bathroom to be right off the master bedroom—a master bathroom. So that's probably your first choice of location.

I've seen homeowners stroll around their master bedroom saying that it should go here, next to the closet, or there next to the window, or someplace else. They consider putting in a whirlpool tub, two sinks, and more. However, arbitrary decisions cost money. More on this in the next section.

What if your home already has two bathrooms and you feel it needs three? Now you may find yourself wanting it to go between two bedrooms. (Typically with two baths, one is in the master bedroom and the other in the hallway.) You can see it fitting nicely between two bedrooms so either can use it conveniently.

The truth is that you can put your new bathroom any place in the house you choose. You can make it as big as you want and add as many features (such as a whirlpool tub) as you like. However, you'd better have a very fat wallet and not care about getting your money back. Adding a new bathroom without scrupulous attention to where you place it (and, hence, keeping costs down) will simply make your home into a white elephant, something that's been so far overimproved that it can't be sold for what the seller has in it.

Add a Cost-Efficient Bathroom

The key to adding a bathroom inexpensively is to work with the existing layout of your home. You're going to need critical connections to hot and cold water and waste drainage. So, go where they already are, next to an existing bathroom. (You can't really put a bathroom on the other side of the wall from a kitchen because the bath needs a four-inch drain for the toilet while the largest drain in a kitchen is usually the two-inch drain from the sink.)

One way to add a bathroom without having to drag pipes great distances is to put it next to an existing bathroom. Check for a closet you can convert, or even a small bedroom, or perhaps part of a larger bedroom. Consider all of the rooms on walls adjacent to the existing bath.

An even more cost-efficient way to add a bathroom is to simply divide your current bathroom into two. This is not as revolutionary an idea as it may sound. Many older homes have few bathrooms but larger ones. Particularly in very old homes there was room for a stand-alone tub plus a stand-alone sink, plus the toilet, and often a linen cabinet. Even in homes built in the 1950s and later, the single bathroom was often fairly large. See if you can divide that single bathroom into two smaller separate bathrooms.

Often, it can be done by having a tub/shower combination with a sink and a toilet in one bathroom and just a toilet and sink in the other. While a toilet/sink-only bathroom is referred to as a half bath in real estate lingo, for most buyers it will suffice as a second bathroom. It increases the value of your home enormously.

The beauty of converting a single bathroom to two is that all of the plumbing is right there. It's usually just a matter of extending pipes, putting in a dividing wall, adding the fixtures and finishing it off. A good-looking bathroom divide can often be done for under $10,000.

A word of caution before beginning, however: Get a good plumber and contractor out to the house not only to give you estimates, but also ideas. If your home is built on a slab, putting in a second bathroom can be outrageously expensive because of the need to crack the concrete and dig. On the other hand, if the new bathroom is to go on the second floor, or if you have a basement or at least a crawl area, it can be a piece of cake.

One final word about quality. Dividing one bathroom into two is cost-efficient, but not necessarily attractive. It will work in a low to moderate-priced home. But, if you have an upscale home, you should consider going to the expense of adding a full, separate bathroom. The price range of the home may well warrant the additional cost.

TECHNIQUE **39**   **$$$**

Convert an attic.

For many homes, the problem is space. The home may be well located, the design may be adequate, however, the house is just too small. If your home had another bedroom or a family room, it would be perfect both for you to live in and for you to sell. That extra room would significantly bump up the price you could get for the property. It would improve your home's value.

This is particularly the case with homes built from the 1950s to the 1980s. At that time, land was generally cheap and plentiful. Hence, builders often put small homes on large lots.

However, after the skyrocketing home prices of the 1980s, the trend changed. Land became more expensive. Hence, builders used far smaller "postage-stamp" sized lots. To compensate for the small lots, they erected huge homes.

Thus, if you have an older home (one built before 1980s), while you may have a great location and a wonderfully big lot, you're in competition with newer homes that are often far bigger. As a result, you'll find your price is significantly knocked down when you try to sell.

The answer is to make your home bigger. One of the easier ways to do this is to convert an existing attic into more living space.

Can It Be Done?

For this technique to work, you must have a suitable attic. Many older homes do, but many do not. You'll need to determine just how well yours will work. And, of course, it should go without saying that before you begin actual work you'll need to get a permit from your local building department.

The first question to consider is ingress and egress—how are you going to get into and out of the attic space? If you already have a stairwell, then it's no problem. However, if you only have a crawl hole to use for getting in, it is a problem. You have to determine where a stairwell can go.

In some homes, this is easy because you have a wide hallway that will accommodate the stairs. (Keep in mind that most building departments will require the stairs to be a minimum of 30 to 36 inches wide.) In other cases, you may need to convert part of a living, family, or dining room to a stairway. However you determine it can be done, be sure that it appears natural. Having access to the attic through a closet in a bedroom is an awkward solution that will not win you cudos from would-be buyers.

Next, check the height of your attic. Most building departments require a minimum of eight feet in height. With a variance, you might get by with seven feet. And in some cases, you can have seven or eight feet in the center sloping down to a minimum of around four or five feet at the sides.

One way to increase the height overall is to add dormers—small areas with windows leading out through the roof. These can be relatively inexpensive to build.

If your existing attic is only five or six feet tall at its highest point, you can probably forget a conversion. You simply don't have the height to pull it off. Don't even dream about increasing the attic's height. This would mean putting on a new roof from the basic structure on up and the cost could be fantastic.

If your existing attic has the ingress and egress as well as the height and area, then it may indeed be a good candidate for conversion. Be sure to call in a contractor to give you ideas of how it might be done as well as cost estimates.

One thing you will want to be very careful to discuss with your contractor is the existing ceiling joists. These are the boards that go across the attic floor and form the support for the ceiling below. While the existing joists may be perfectly adequate for supporting a ceiling, they may be completely *inadequate* for supporting an attic floor. That means the contractor will either have to replace them or more likely, add additional support. Now you'll have to get engineering help.

A structural engineer will be able to calculate the size of joist required to support your attic floor according to the local building department requirements. It could be as little as 40 pounds per square foot or as much as a hundred. He or she will also be able to determine whether the existing side walls of the home can support the weight of the new floor (usually they can).

Finally, your contractor will have to figure out how to support the existing roof without the bracing typically found in the attic. These are beams that go from the joists up to the attic peak and help hold it up. Without these beams, additional side bracing will be needed. Should your home have high-tech truss construction, then no solution may be possible because it's not usually feasible to change these supports in any way.

Sound like a formidable chore? It can be, depending on what your attic now looks like. However, in many cases, solutions can be found. And when they can, the attic conversion can often be accomplished quickly and inexpensively. Remember, the basic floors, walls, and ceiling are already in place. All that's needed is to strengthen and finish them off, where possible.

What about the Finish Work?

In addition to the basic structure, there's also the electrical and finish work that's required. The electrical work involves putting in plugs (most building departments require them every 12 feet along the periphery of all walls), switches, and lights. An electrician should be able to do this by tapping into your existing circuits in a matter of a day or less. Do not attempt to do this yourself unless you're competent to handle the job. Few people are.

The finish work usually means having professionals come in to sheetrock the new room, tape it, and texture it. Then there's the matter of windows, doors, and finish molding.

If you plan it well, do some of the work yourself, and don't run into too many problems, you can often finish off the conversion for $10,000 to $15,000. At the same time, you may add significantly to the value of your home.

A word of caution: Many people want to add not one room, but several. If you have the space, there's nothing wrong with that, unless one of those rooms is a new bathroom. If that's the case, then turn back to the last technique to see what some of the concerns are. Adding a new room and bathroom will certainly add value to the home. But running the plumbing to the new bathroom can significantly increase the cost of the conversion.

Converting attic space to an additional room can be a worthwhile way of adding value to your home. Just be sure that it looks professionally done. A slapped together job that looks like something "that Jack built," can just as easily lower the value of your property.

$$$

Finish off a basement.

In those parts of the country where basements are common, finishing one off is often an inexpensive way to add value to your property. After all, the basement is already there. You have the floor, walls, and at least part of the ceiling. What could be easier?

The problem is how the final product looks. Does it seem like a natural part of the house? Does the traffic flow to the basement blend in with that of the house proper? Is it well finished?

Or, is it a dank, dark hole that looks like a car garage made over? Too often basements have been finished off to look like depressions in the ground where no one would want to go. Instead of fulfilling their intended purpose of adding value to the property, they actually detract from it. Buyers subtract the money they figure it will cost them to do a good job of finishing off the basement. That's typically far, far more than it ever would cost you to do it.

The rule here is that if you're going to finish off a basement, do it right. And, of course, get a building permit before you start. You'll need to declare to future buyers whether or not the work was done with permit and it avoids many complications to be able to prove that it was.

Plan on Spending Money

Because most basements already have the structural (and sometimes the electrical and plumbing) work in place, the natural tendency is to think you can do the finish work for pocket change. Rather than create a budget, you just figure you'll spend whatever it costs out of your regularly budgeted money.

That's usually a mistake. Even with all the structure in place, finishing off a basement properly usually involves dry walling it, adding molding, finishing the electrical work, lighting, carpeting, adding doors and windows, perhaps adding a bathroom, and more. A typical budget for finishing off a basement can easily come to $10,000 and often it is much more. If you're going to do it, plan on doing it right and that means having the money available. (Home remodeling loans were designed just for this purpose and are readily available.)

Walls and Floors

What makes a basement finish job looks bad is usually two things. The first is the break between the "cripple," the short wall supporting the house between the foundation and the first floor, and the basement cement walls. The basement wall is often wood, perhaps a third of the way down, with the remaining two-thirds concrete wall. The transition from wood to concrete in the walls needs to be handled so that it doesn't show. Too often would-be finishers will simply attempt to add drywall directly to the wood, put a border around, and then simply paint the cement. I've never seen this kind of job look professionally done.

Actually, what needs to be done is to fir pieces of support lumber (typically 2 by 4s) from floor to ceiling in front of the combo wood/cement cement walls of the basement thus creating a secondary wall a few inches in. The firred lumber then can be nailed to the wood and into the cement producing a solid base for installing drywall. Thus, when the drywall is attached, it gives the appearance of a perfectly normal wall, a polished look.

The same holds true with the floor. Often linoleum is laid right on top of the cement floor of the basement. However, that floor typically is uneven. What's worse, it may never have had a impermeable membrane laid beneath it (or the membrane may leak) meaning that moisture can well up loosening the linoleum flooring. The result is an uneven floor with bubbles and/or buckles. It looks terrible.

The correct way to handle the basement floor is to treat the cement as a base-floor and put a subfloor above it. This can take many forms from pouring new concrete with an impermeable membrane beneath it to laying a wood floor on top. However you do it, the final level floor will be able to accept linoleum, carpeting, tile, or whatever flooring you choose for a professional finished look. (An additional advantage of creating a subfloor is that you may want to install a floor heating system that will remove the dank feeling often found in basements.)

Dealing with Ceilings

The easiest thing to do with ceilings is to simply insulate, put in whatever wiring and heating ductwork is necessary, and drywall. However, the big problem is that often basements are subheight. That means that instead of the normal eight feet, you've got a seven and a half foot or even lower ceiling. If that's the case, you'll need to run down to your building department to see if you can get a variance to convert your basement. With a ceiling too low, it may simply not be possible to do it.

Lighting

Another big problem with basements is that they frequently lack windows. Or, if they do have windows, these are shorter than normal, often only a foot tall, and are at ground height. While they may let in some air and light, they are often shrouded by landscaping and are not really adequate for lighting the basement. Therefore, plan on putting in plenty of artificial light.

The best installed lighting in basements that I have seen is recessed lighting. These are simple to install at the time of the conversion by locating the metal boxes between ceiling joists. Since they do not intrude into the room, they do not accent any height problems the basement may have. And you can install a whole host of them all across the basement, lighting it up like daylight.

Recessed lighting is relatively inexpensive when it comes to materials—the big cost is the electrician. Don't do it yourself unless you're competent to handle electrical work and, as I remind you every time electricity is involved, turn off *all* power before doing any such work.

There is a tendency to use fluorescent lighting in basements because it's so easy to install (just one electrical box needed per light) and just one or two can give loads of light. However, to my way of thinking, this is a mistake. Fluorescents have a green cast. While our minds color correct this to white, the effect remains subliminally and it makes the basement room feel more like a commercial building.

Finish It Off

The final finish work in a basement should be up to the same standards as the house. Use the same quality molding, doors, handles, paint, and fixtures.

You want the basement to flow naturally from the house. You want it to seem as though it was designed to be a part of the home. If you succeed, you'll have added real value, at nominal cost.

TECHNIQUE **41**   **$**

Organize closets.

When many of us first put our home up for sale we make the mistake of thinking that potential buyers will never look in the closets. We think of closets as our personal space, hence, why would a buyer poke around in there? It's off limits, isn't it?

No, it's not. Buyers purchase the whole house and that includes the closets. You can be sure that once they are seriously interested in your place, they will open every closet door, walk into every closet, and make judgments about how much space the closets offer.

Buyers are not concerned with how many clothes you have or their quality. They're concerned with how many clothes they have and where they will put them. They are looking for storage space, and how your closets appear will tell them a great deal.

For example, let's say that you've cleaned up your home so that it will show well. However, in so doing you took all those extra knick-knacks that were in the living, dining, and family rooms and crammed them into your closets. When the would-be buyer opens the closet doors, they tumble out. Your closets are packed to bursting.

Now, what does that tell the buyer? Does it suggest that you have all sorts of storage space that will accommodate the buyer's things? Or does it send the message that your home simply doesn't have enough room? If there's not enough storage space for your stuff, how will the buyers ever fit all their stuff in? Perhaps the answer is to get a different house with bigger closets?

In short, you can lose a deal or get a lower offer simply because your closets are bulging. To get more money and a faster offer for your home, there are some things you can do.

Closet Improvements

- *Remove 50 percent of everything from every closet.* It doesn't really matter where you put it, as long as it's not in your house (or garage). Store your stuff at a relative's or friend's house, rent a storage space, whatever. Just get it out of your closet.
- *Paint your closets white.* White makes anything seem larger. With less of your clothing and other articles in the closet, there will be more white space. And it will appear that you have more closet space than you may actually have.
- *On each rack, hang only enough clothing to fill half the rack.* The half that's empty will make the closet look huge. It will suggest to would-be buyers that there's plenty of room to hang their items.
- *Remove everything from closet shelves.* You might want to leave a small blanket or box up there to show that you are using the space, but make sure it appears that there's loads of room for storing the buyer's boxes and other items. Paint the shelves white, too. Use a glossy white that will shine.
- *Be sure the closet smells fresh.* Odors from clothes and shoes can permeate a closet. When the would-be buyers open the closet door, they can be hit with smells that turn them off not only to the closet, but to your home. Air out closets, remove smelly clothes, and use products

such as Febreze to absorb odors and give the closet a fresh smell.

Build in Closet Organizers

Nothing makes a closet look better than to have shelves, drawers, racks for shoes, and other organizing features. Indeed, there are some buyers who consider this a huge plus and are willing to pay more for it. However, they are not usually willing to pay much more.

Rather, a closet organizer helps convince the buyer that yours is a quality home, a place where they would love to put their things. A place where they would love to live. In other words, it's a strong selling feature, though not necessarily one that will yield you a big return.

All of which is to interject a word of caution about spending big bucks on closet organizers. You can hire someone to come out and makeover your closet and easily drop $5,000 or more in the process. If you do that, don't expect to get your money back.

On the other hand, if you can get someone who knows how to organize closets to give you some advice on how to handle yours, you can do much of it yourself. Stores that specialize in closet organization will often send a professional out to analyze your closets either for free or for a small fee. Take what they say seriously and if they offer to do the work for a small amount of money, say around $500, consider doing it.

On the other hand, if it's much more, consider doing it yourself. Most home supply stores sell shelving, drawers, and all the other ingredients necessary to do a closet makeover. However, be sure you know what you want (remember, get advice given by an expert) before you buy and try to install, or else you could simply be wasting money and end up with items that are too big, too small, or inappropriate for your closet.

Are They Hard to Install?

Since much of the closet organizing materials sold at home supply stores is made either out of steel or pressed wood, the biggest problem you're likely to have with it is weight. It tends to weigh a ton!

However, the assembly and installation is quite simple. I've done it myself on several occasions and know others who have done it as well. Usually only a screwdriver is needed. A word to the wise, however: Try to assemble it as close as possible to the area where it will eventually end up. Moving it after it's assembled can be difficult (because of the weight) and can sometimes cause it to break.

One final note: Most of the do-it-yourself closet organizers come in stark white. There's nothing wrong with this and in a closet, as noted above, it can help to make things look bigger. However, you may also want to paint it so that it adds an accent. Just be sure to use mild colors. Deep purples, blues, and so on will only make your closet look weird . . . and small.

Finally, don't overstuff the organizers with clothes. Just as buyers will open closet doors, so too will they open drawers. Fill everything no more than half full.

Closets are a surprisingly important feature of every house. Be sure that yours add to its value.

TECHNIQUE **42** $$

Convert a bedroom.

What would sell for more money—a five-bedroom house or a four-bedroom house? Without any other information, the correct answer is presumably the five-bedroom house. More bedrooms means more value. But, does it really?

If we're talking about a mansion with each bedroom being the size of a football field, then certainly yes, more is better in terms of value. But, what if we're talking of a more modest home where each of the bedrooms is closet-sized? In other words, what if the home is really too small to accommodate five bedrooms? In that case, a home that was the same size, but with four or even three larger bedrooms could sell for more, and could certainly sell quicker.

Think of it as if you were a builder. You have 2,000 square feet to play with. Into those square feet you can place bedrooms each taking 200 square feet (including closets). How many bedrooms should you put into your house?

If you put in three bedrooms, you have roughly 1,400 square feet left into which you can put living areas plus bathrooms, kitchen, and hallways. And you can increase the size of the master bedroom.

But, if you have five bedrooms at 200 square feet apiece, you only have room for about 1,000 square feet for the rest of the house, including living areas. Increase the size of the master bedroom and there's even less area.

The point is that some homes have too many rooms for their square footage. This is often the case with tract houses in which builders create different home packages, all roughly the same square footage, but some with more bedrooms and some with less. Often the homes with more bedrooms suffer.

Fifty years ago, typical home buyers had bigger families and were looking for more rooms in the house. Today, home buyers have smaller families (and many are empty nesters) and are looking for more living area. This is particularly the case when, over time, a neighborhood becomes increasingly upscale.

If your home lacks living area and has many small bedrooms, you may want to convert one or more.

What Can I Convert a Bedroom Into?

It all depends, of course, on the design and flow of your home. But the two most common conversions are to make two small bedrooms into one large master bedroom suite. Or, to open a wall between a living/family room and a bedroom to make a much larger living area.

Keep in mind, however, that every home is different. And converting a bedroom into another use often requires creativity. Check which rooms are adjacent to the rooms you want to convert.

Don't limit your thinking. What you're actually doing is re-designing your home. It may very well pay to call in a architect for a consultation to give you ideas. Sometimes an interior decorator can also suggest options. Be flexible. Think about what requires the least costly approach. This is a case where doing less often results in accomplishing more.

What's Involved in Converting a Bedroom?

Remember, you're not adding square footage to your home. You're simply rearranging it. Therefore, what's usually involved is removing a wall here and there, creating a new doorway, and possibly adding a window.

With walls, the critical issue is whether it's a load-bearing wall or not. A load-bearing wall is one that supports the roof or the ceiling. Most interior walls are not bearing walls, which means you can knock them out without affecting the structure of the house. On the other hand, if you want to move a bearing wall, you may need to reinforce the ceiling and roof, something that can be quite expensive.

The easiest way to understand why most interior walls are not load-bearing is to see a house under construction in the framing stage. Find a house that is at this stage and stop by to take a closer look. Typically, the roof is supported by the exterior walls. If the framing uses truss construction (the most common today), so too does the interior ceiling. Then the rooms are created by having carpenters put up wall panels wherever the plans call for them. The walls are nailed into place to form the rooms of the house. As a result, it is relatively easy to knock walls out to expand one room into two (not really too easy, because you still have to deal with the sheet rock on top of them as well as any plumbing and electrical wiring that runs through them).

To know if a wall in your home is bearing or not, take a look in your attic (assuming you have one). If there are no boards leading from the top of the wall to the roof, the wall probably doesn't support the roof. If you have roof trusses (factory built supports for roof and ceiling), chances are the wall doesn't provide ceiling support either. Even with trusses, the wall may contribute to ceiling support. To be sure, you should have a contractor come to your home to give you a definitive answer.

How Do I Cut Costs?

We're talking about a major makeover and there are many ways to go about it. As noted earlier, if you stick only to nonbearing walls, you will have cut your total costs by half if not more.

If you knock out walls between two rooms that logically go together (such as a small bedroom next to a small master bedroom or a small bedroom next to a family room), virtually the only work you'll need to do is removing the wall and then finishing the work.

However, as also noted, be wary of electrical wiring and plumbing (usually found in walls near bathrooms, kitchens, and utility rooms) that might go through a wall. It's usually fairly easy to reroute electrical wiring. However, rerouting plumbing can be a major concern. Remember, water flows downward and all plumbing is based on this whether it be drains or vents. Just one vent pipe coming up through a wall may require thousands of dollars in plumbing work to have it moved.

Doing it yourself will save you more money. But, just keep in mind that you'll need a building permit for this and expertise in plumbing, electrical work, and framing. Sometimes hiring it out can be cheaper in the long run.

Finally, you'll need to refinish the new room. This includes adding new electrical sockets and/or switches, patching the sheetrock, texturing, taping, and painting. You'll also need to put a new floor in the new room.

I've seen people do these kinds of conversions for as little as $1,500 and as much as $15,000 or more. Of course, the less you spend and more dramatic the result (in a positive way), the more you can add to the value of your home.

TECHNIQUE **43** $$

Add an extra room.

This is one area where I almost always recommend that home-owners do not go. Adding space is usually the most costly thing you can do for your house.

On the other hand, in some homes, adding a room can be a necessity. Where needed, it can dramatically increase value. Of course, the trick is to know when it's needed and when it's not.

When Do I Need to Add a Room?

There are many reasons that owners want to add a room to their homes. They include:

- *Family has expanded.* You need another bedroom for the kids.
- *Want more living space.* You would like to have a library or additional family room.
- *Heard it was a good idea.* You read in a magazine that adding a room was relatively easy and would add to your property's value.
- *Your home is too small.*

Interestingly, none of these reasons, except the last one, make financial sense. The only time it makes sense, economically, to add a room is if your home is too small. Then it's important to understand how "being too small" is defined.

I define it as having a home that's got structural obsolescence. What I mean by that is that the home is simply smaller than the homes that the majority of buyers are looking for.

For example, in the 1950s and 1960s, many homes were built that were 1,000 to 1,200 square feet in size. Often they had three bedrooms, two baths, a living room, dining "L," kitchen, and family room all crowded into this small space. At the time, they were considered minimalist, but adequate. Considering that they originally sold for $8,000 to $12,000, many GIs using their veteran's benefits felt they were just right.

But by today's standards, they are simply too small. Today, most people begin looking at houses that start around 1,500 square feet at minimum and go up from there. Those older homes are simply too small to compete in today's market-place—except that they are frequently in great locations and they are built on huge lots. These are features that today's buyers would love to have, but which are seldom offered by newer home construction.

Thus, adding on a room or two to one of those smaller houses (along with a general remodel) can often boost those homes out of their low-cost status into homes that have moderate or even upscale potential. Depending on where the home is located, what you add, and how well you do the job, you can sometimes multiply the amount of money you put into the project when you sell!

There's another case when adding on space makes sense. You're in an area of largely custom homes. All the homes around you are 2,500 square feet. Your home is only 1,800 square feet. When you try to sell, your price is knocked down significantly (perhaps a quarter or a third or more) because of the smaller size of your home. (Of course, you probably paid a third or so less when you bought.)

Now add on. Suddenly your home becomes competitive with its neighbors. All else being equal, you can jump the price up by that quarter to a third, which may be more than the cost of adding that extra room.

Thus, it makes sense to add on when your home is basically too small for the tastes of buyers, or too small when compared to surrounding properties. However, unless these two conditions exist, you're probably better off leaving your home its current size.

What's Involved with Adding On?

It's major construction from the ground up. It's the exact same process you'd go through if you were building a new home from scratch.

If you think you'll be saving because part of the addition is attached to the existing home, think again. Tearing out existing construction and then adding on new is usually far *more* expensive.

While the costs will vary depending on the quality of work, how much renovation is needed, and the area of the country, it would not be unexpected to pay $100 to $150 a square foot and higher. That means to add on only 100 square feet (a very small 10-foot × 10-foot bedroom) would cost $10,000 to $15,000. To add 400 square feet (roughly the size of a small garage) could cost $40,000 to $60,000. As I said, adding on can be expensive.

Where Do Add-Ons Work Best?

It depends largely on the style and layout of your home. However, those additions that I've see work particularly well include the following:

- *Expanding a master bathroom.* Perhaps only 40 to 50 square feet are added, however, this gives you room to install a whirlpool bath and other amenities, thus making the bathroom appear upscale.

- *Adding to the size of the main living area.* Here you could be making a living or dining room larger. The extra space makes the house appear far more spacious.
- *Adding an extra bedroom.* This only works when the house has an inadequate number of bedrooms. For example, some homes have only two bedrooms, sometimes composed of two master suites. For a particular buyer, this works well. But most buyers demand that extra bedroom for guests, children, and so on. Adding it opens your home to a much larger market.

Contract It Out or Do It Yourself?

If you're a carpenter or otherwise in the building trades, then by all means consider doing it yourself. You already know what's required and have many of the skills it takes.

On the other hand, if you've never done any construction work, then stay away. Not only will it cost you more to learn on the job, but chances are you'll end up with an inferior looking product (not to mention all those back sprains!).

For those who're are in between, I suggest you check out some of the many books on the subject that explain exactly what's involved and how to do it. Books I have written on the subject include, *Tips & Traps When Renovating Your Home,* and *Tips & Traps When Building Your Own Home,* (McGraw-Hill, 2000).

TECHNIQUE **44**   **$**

Install double-pane windows.

Ten years ago (or even five), I would never have mentioned this as a technique for increasing the value of your home. The reason is that, though beneficial, buyers back then simply wouldn't pay extra for a home with this feature.

Today, however, with nationwide concern about climatic changes and even more concern with energy costs, this has become a realistic option. Today, buyers look for homes whose energy efficiency has been upgraded. It's something you should think about if your home is older and only has single-pane windows.

First, a little background. Glass windows have been used in homes for hundreds of years. They are excellent at keeping out wind and pests and at the same time allowing us to see the sun, the sky, and everything outside our home. Indeed, it's almost unthinkable to have a home without windows.

Glass windows, however, at least the old-fashioned single-pane variety are terrible at keeping out heat or cold. Indeed, they are almost perfect transmitters. The ability to resist heat transmission is called the R-factor. The insulation put in the attic of many homes is often rated at R-34. The higher the rating the better.

The R-factor for a typical single-pane glass window is R-1. (This means that the attic insulation offers 34 times more heat resistance than glass!)

When you install double-pane glass, you cut heat transmission in half, from R-1 to R-2. (That may not seem like a lot, but remember, it's cutting your heat loss by 50 percent.) By including special thermal coatings on the glass known as Lo-E (low emissivity) you can increase the rating to R-6 or R-7.

The difference is striking. A display commonly found in shops that sell glass is to have a heat lamp on one side of a piece of single-pane glass. When you put your hand to the glass, you can easily feel the heat. In fact, it's almost too warm to touch. Then the lamp is put behind a piece of double-pane Lo-E glass. When you touch the glass, it's cool, almost no heat radiating through. Take this test and it will make you a believer!

The big advantage of double-pane Lo-E glass is that it keeps the heat out in summer and the heat in winter. Today, where temperature extremes are rapidly becoming the rule rather than the exception in so many parts of the country, double-pane Lo-E glass is becoming well known and desired.

What about Appearance?

The second reason for installing double-pane windows has to do with their appearance. This, possibly even more than their effectiveness at controlling temperature, is boosting their popularity.

Take a look at the windows in your home. Look not at the glass, but at the window frames. If your home is more than 10 or 15 years old, chances are the window frames are made of aluminum, steel, or wood. And chances are also good that if frames are aluminum, it's oxidized and has an unsightly white coating on it. If steel, it's also oxidized and that coating is red rust, often bleeding through paint. And if wood, there's probably some rot and peeling paint.

Now, try opening and closing those windows. It's rare that they will work smoothly. The oxidization, rot, and sometimes the shifting of the house over time will help to bind the windows. This is particularly the case with single-pane aluminum windows.

As a result, your present windows may not work well, but even more important when it comes time to sell, they may look bad. And remember, appearance is critical to getting a good price for your home.

Modern Double-Pane Windows Look Good

Today's modern double-pane window frames are typically made out of plastic (PVC). There are also wood versions available and some of the most expensive incorporate steel encased in wood. They all look terrific.

My personal favorite are the plastic frame variety. The frames are usually white (although they are available in several other colors) and they are wide, so they can be prominently seen. The latches are well made and the windows slide perfectly almost every time. They are resistant to shifts in the house, so they should continue to slide well for years. Most important of all, they are readily available as retrofits.

Can I Easily Replace My Old Windows?

Companies such as Milgard (www.milgard.com) offer retrofit windows that require minimal installation and don't demand that you rip out any existing construction. The procedure for installing them starts with precise measurements of the inside dimensions of your existing window frame.

These measurements are then sent to the factory where windows are cut precisely to fit your frame holes. They are then delivered to your home where either you or a professional can install them.

The new plastic frame windows look great. They are clean, bold, and catch attention. You can't miss them when you walk into the house . . . and neither will buyers.

How Much Do They Cost?

That's the rub. Because retrofit windows are made to fit, they are expensive. While you might be able to buy a new-construction double-pane window in a standard size at a building supply store for around a hundred dollars, it can easily cost $300 to $500 for the retrofit, installed. Of course, if you were to buy a new-construction window, it would require that you break out the old, and then refinish the interior and exterior, something which can cost far more than a retrofit.

A typical house will cost $6,000 to $8,000 to retrofit with double-pane windows. A lot depends on how many sliders (sliding glass doors) you have since these are far more expensive, sometimes as much as $1,000 apiece.

You can opt for high-tech wood frames. However, the price is often significantly higher.

The big question is: Will doing this really improve the value of my home. The likelihood increases when you live in areas of the country with extremes of heat or cold. It's something to consider when your old windows are single-pane, unsightly, or do not work. (I've even seen homeowners replace double-pane windows with the newer models to get the benefit of better appearance and lower heat transmission from Lo-E.)

$

Replace interior doors.

Anything you can do to boost the appearance of your home, to make it look more upscale and less downscale to a buyer, can result in an increase in value. It's the old story of selling the sizzle and not the steak. One of the easiest and least expensive techniques is to change out the doors inside your home.

Today's modern upscale homes offer handsome interior doors. They come in a variety of designs and materials and, when a new and modern handle is attached, add class to a home. In fact, you can almost always tell the difference between a new tract home and an older one by the quality of the interior doors.

If you live in an older tract home, you may already know what I mean. The doors that lead to bedrooms, closets, and elsewhere inside the home are simply flat. They have a tiny area of molding around them (see Technique 32 for changing out molding), and they tend to look cheap. That's because they usually are.

In older tract homes, interior doors are typically hollow core. They are made by creating a frame of wood (usually pine) and then gluing a thin veneer of wood or masonite (if they're going to be painted) on that frame. Cardboard is often used to add support in the hollow core. You can buy these doors today at building supply stores for around $25, sometimes less.

Modern designer doors, on the other hand, are three-dimensional. They may still be hollow core, but the outer skin is often made of fiberglass. When painted, they look like the heavy wooden doors made a century ago of layered wood. They are still relatively inexpensive, under a $100 and often under $50.

Of course, there's also the cost of a new handle and the hanging (which with prehung doors is relatively simple). Nonetheless, you can often replace your interior doors for as little as $100 apiece. That's probably less than a thousand dollars in materials cost for the entire home. And the value added by the better appearance is generally more than that.

What Is Involved in Replacing Doors?

It all depends on whether you want to do it yourself or if you want to hire it out. If you want to hire it out, you'll need a carpenter to hang the doors. Often the stores that sell the doors can recommend an installer. Then it's simply a matter of getting the installer to give you a bid (in writing), buying the doors, having them delivered, and then having the carpenter install them. Installation can run as high as $100 a door.

Or you can do it yourself and save a bundle. It's not hard. I've done it countless times, especially using "prehung" where the door and jamb all come together. But, be sure you're up to it. Moving these doors around is not light work and getting them installed plumb can be tricky. Get a book to guide you.

What about Painting?

The doors we've been describing need to be painted. You can get a variety of doors in natural woods that can be stained, but the price skyrockets. There's no point in hanging new doors if you don't finish the job right. And painting or staining is the finish work. You can either hire a painter to do the work, or handle it yourself.

What about Cabinet Doors?

In addition to room doors, there are also doors that go to linen cabinets, furnace compartments, and other areas. You can change these out at the same time as you do the room doors. However, be aware that it may be difficult to find replacement doors that match the sizes you have. Cabinet doors are sometimes built to order and that means that your only alternative would be to get new ones custom made—a very expensive proposition.

Changing out doors is one of those things which can be done inexpensively, yet which can add class to your home. And class is often reflected in a higher price.

Note: When replacing doors that lead to a garage, building departments usually require they be solid core and that they close by themselves (spring loaded). This is to provide protection in case of a garage fire and to keep car fumes out of the house. Also, all exterior doors should be solid core for security reasons.

Techniques That Work in the Backyard

$

Landscape low in your backyard.

There are two ways to landscape a backyard. One is to do it to please yourself. The other is to do it for effect, in other words, to please others, namely potential buyers.

Before we begin, however, it's important to understand that no matter what you do to your backyard, it won't yield you much in return. Consider what builders do when they put up model homes to promote the sale of their tract houses.

Typically model homes have elaborate backyards with fountains, rock gardens, and sometimes pools and spas (which we'll go into in Techniques 48 and 49). Spacious lawns, exotic plants, decks, and overhangs are the rule. In short, the back-yards for model homes are often elaborate and beautiful. When you gaze at them from the house, it's easy to imagine yourself amidst all that beauty. And that, of course, is the effect they are supposed to produce.

While it's nothing for a builder to sink $10,000 to $20,000 into the model home backyard, keep in mind that the builder is trying to impress you. He or she is showing you just what you, too, can do if you buy one of these homes, what your backyard could look like.

But it won't. I've never seen a tract home where the backyard was included in the price of the home. In fact, in most cases, the backyard isn't even an upgrade that's offered to buyers. You can upgrade to better carpets, to better kitchen counters, to better fixtures. But, upgrade to a landscaped backyard? At best, there'll be a sign posted in the backyard telling you which landscape company put the model yard in so that you can contact them yourself.

Buyers seldom want to purchase backyard landscaping. They almost always figure it's something they can do themselves later on . . . yet they seldom do it. The moral here is that landscaped backyards help sell homes. But, they add only minimally to the price you can ask for those homes.

If you put in a minimal amount of money, time, and effort into your backyard, you will help sell your home and probably get enough boost in price to warrant the work. However, if you do extensive landscaping, just consider it money spent to please yourself. Although it will help sell your home faster, it won't impress buyers enough to pay much more for it.

What Should I Do?

Consider the backyard in terms of low and high landscaping. In this technique, we consider low landscaping. This refers to planting vegetation and putting in low decking.

Let's assume that you've done nothing to your backyard. That it's got weeds that are three feet tall that you need a machete just to break trail in order to work you way through to the back fence or the end of your lot. Buyers who take a look at this will knock down the price of your home. They'll figure it will cost them several thousand dollars to clean up the backyard and put it into shape.

Here, it's easy to make an improvement that will prevent this. Simply cut the weeds. If you do nothing other than clean up the yard, you'll add value. Rent a weed eater and for about $50 you'll add a significant amount to your home's value. At the least, you'll most certainly get a quicker sale.

If you want to move a step up from this, then rent a roto-tiller and turn over the ground. Use a roller to flatten it and buy 50 dollars worth of seed. Spread it out, cover with a thin layer of soil, and water the heck out of it.

Two weeks later, you should have the beginnings of a lawn and in a few months it will be lush and green. Keep mowing and watering it and soon it will become lush and inviting. For little more than a hundred dollars, you've probably added a thousand or more to the value of your home (or at least kept it from being knocked down by that much).

From here, however, it gets harder. To keep a lawn going, you really need a good watering system, meaning sprinklers. (See Technique 3.) That can cost anywhere from a few hundred dollars (if you do it yourself), up to several thousand dollars to hire a professional to install it. You won't get much more for your professionally installed system when you sell the house than if your simply drag a hose out and do the watering yourself.

You may also want to plant low flowers and shrubs around the periphery of your lot. The cost of these plants is minimal, particularly if you buy them when they are very small and allow them to grow. After a year or so, they develop into beautiful hedges, flower beds, and other decorative areas. Now buyers who come by will be even more impressed, will tend to make more offers, and may even offer ever so slightly more. Just re-member, however, that you'll be out there hand watering every day or so unless you install an automatic watering system.

Finally, you can put in a patio or deck. Decks are highly desirable. They give you a place to entertain and to cook outdoors, something that's definitely a plus. A deck can add value to a home. However, don't expect a buyer to pay you for what it will cost you to add that deck.

So, if you must have a deck, consider doing it the cheapest way possible. The typical deck or patio is constructed of wood or concrete. On the other hand, paving stones or bricks make an acceptable deck without much cost and effort. Simply level the soil, put down some gravel to even it out, and then put in the paving stones or bricks. Voila, you've got your deck.

Alternatively, you can put in a wooden or cement deck. These are typically raised a foot or so above the ground. However, they require footings, supports, joists, and, of course, decking. Wood decking that's resistant to mold, such as redwood or cedar, has become incredibly expensive. A simple 10-foot by 15-foot wood deck (150 square feet) can easily cost $5,000 installed.

What If I Already Have a Nice Backyard?

Chances are it was either put in by someone who owned the house before you, or you already spent some money on it. If so, then you have it made. Simply clean, trim, and spruce it up. You may want to treat your patio or deck with stain or sealant to improve its appearance. Wood can be water-pressure cleaned and then stained. Bricks, stone, and cement can be chemically treated to remove stains in most cases.

Backyards need to look neat, clean, and livable. Just remember, however, that spending a lot of money on them is like digging a money pit.

TECHNIQUE **47** $

Landscape high in your backyard.

Unless you happen to have a dynamite view from your back-yard, what most people want is privacy. They want to be able to go into their backyard and have a picnic, to sit in the sun, to have the children play, and so on and do it all without having the neighbors looking in on them.

In those parts of the country, primarily the Midwest and parts of the East, where open spaces and no fences are the rule, this is somewhat hard to achieve. But even so, with the proper planting of taller trees and bushes, at least a portion of the yard can provide a strong sense of privacy.

Adding height in the backyard also makes it seem larger. Trees and taller bushes add spaciousness to a backyard in much the same way taller ceilings do in a house. It forces the viewer (the potential buyer) to look up and take in the three-dimensional area instead of just looking down at the lawn. A few strategically placed trees can make a small backyard seem to have vistas.

Finally, there's the matter of shade. Well-placed trees can shade a house in the summer and reduce air-conditioning costs. Sitting in the shade of a beautiful oak or magnolia tree in the summer while sipping a drink is one of life's nicer pleasures.

These factors—space, privacy, and shade—are going to in-fluence what a buyer will be willing to pay. Keep in mind, we're not saying that putting in elaborate landscaping is going to get you a pumped up price. But, putting in thoughtful landscaping to emphasize space and private areas can improve the sales potential of your house.

Beware of a "Fenced In" Look

The tendency is to buy tall trees and plant them all along the periphery of the property. The result is that instead of showing off spaciousness, it will overshadow the yard—emphasizing the lack of space. Tall trees will dwarf a tiny plot of grass and perhaps the deck that they surround. They may increase privacy but they work against spaciousness. You don't want to create the impression that you've got a little cottage in a giant, dark forest. You'll just scare buyers away.

Rather, if you're going to go for taller trees, plant them in clumps or groves. Three groupings is usually the maximum, one for each side of the backyard. And be sure there's plenty of open space between them so a would-be buyer can see out as well as up.

Pay Attention to Height

If you hire a professional landscaper to do your backyard, you should have no problem here. Any competent landscaper or gardener will select trees and bushes whose heights compliment the home and yard. For example, if your home is single story, chances are you won't want any trees that are much more than 20 feet tall. That's a little above the height of a typical roof peak in a single-story home (usually 15 to 17 feet). If you have a flat roof, then you'll want to limit trees to around 10 or 12 feet, again to match the height of your roof.

On the other hand, if you have a two-story, or even a three-story home, then taller trees will work better. Putting in shorter trees will only make the house itself look awkward.

Pay Attention to the Type of Tree

I recently bought a home in which the previous owner had planted pine trees in the backyard. These are tall, wide trees that are reminiscent of a mountain landscape. They also tend to remind people of the wilderness, where they are frequently found.

The house itself was single story, but at the time I bought it, the trees were at least 40 feet tall and growing taller every day. They dwarfed the house. Indeed, you could pick out the house from blocks away by the trees. In part I bought the home because of the trees. They gave the place such an awkward look that the seller was forced to reduce the price. I got it for a song.

In speaking to a neighbor, I was told that the former owner had bought the pine trees because they looked so cute when they were small. They had only been about three feet tall when planted. They continued to be attractive as they grew until they reached about 15 feet. If they had stopped there, they would at least not have detracted from the property. But they continued to grow until they became an eyesore.

All of which is to say, be very careful of what type of tall trees you plant. Pine trees, are often chosen because they grow quickly and, in a few years, can be 10 or 15 feet tall, providing a pleasant appearance, shade, and privacy. However, as was my case, many varieties grow to heights of as much as a hundred feet. True, it could take them 20 or more years to do so, but at that time they would tower over not only your house, but your entire neighborhood!

A good choice for many backyards is fruit trees. Today, nurseries typically will tell you the maximum width and height the tree is likely to achieve. There are many varieties of dwarf fruit trees available. You can select the trees you want based on their ultimate size, the amount of shade they give, the color of the flowers they produce, and even the fruit they bear. Used sparingly, they provide an excellent way to inexpensively go tall in your backyard.

Remove Unsightly Trees

Which brings us to another subject, removing trees that are inappropriate for your backyard. Unless you've just moved into a brand new home where the backyard was never landscaped, chances are you already have trees growing there. Many of these, as just noted, may simply be too tall or otherwise inappropriate. When that's the case, don't hesitate to remove them.

A word of caution, however—if they're tall, hire a professional to remove them. Tree removal can be very dangerous work. You may think it's simply a matter of buying a chain saw and making a couple of cuts. However, if you cut wrong and the tree falls on you . . . or your neighbor's roof, you'll rue the day you decided to do it on your own. Unfortunately, the professionals charge $500 to $1,000 per tall tree. But, they have the knowledge to do it right, and should have the insurance to protect you if they make a mistake. (Any good tree removal professional will show you a current policy of liability insurance for at least a million dollars or more.)

_____

Note: Some cities and counties have restrictions on tree removal. They feel that trees contribute to the overall beauty of the community and, in order to remove them, even when they are on your own property, you need a permit. Presumably you will be given permission, but if the tree is a protected species, you may not be able to remove it, even if you consider it an eyesore.

Do not cut a tree nor even trim a tree that is on your neighbor's property. In some states, the penalty is severe. In California, for example, if you cut down your neighbor's tree without permission, you could be liable for three times the cost of planting a new, similar tree!

TECHNIQUE **48** $

Add a spa.

Adding a spa is very controversial. Many real estate agents say that you can never recoup the money it costs, let alone have it increase the value of your property. I disagree, provided certain conditions are present. (By the way, for those who aren't familiar with them, spas are like small swimming pools, typically holding around 500 gallons of water, and with the ability to heat up to very warm temperatures and produce bubbling, swirling waters—they are considered a marvelous way to relax.)

In some areas, spas are the rule rather than the exception. If you're on the East Coast or in the South, a spa may be considered a luxury, even an excess. But, if you're on the West Coast or the Southwest, a spa is often considered more of a necessity. And people are willing to pay more for a home that has one.

It's important not to pay a fortune for putting in a spa. An in-ground installation can easily cost $15,000 or more. On the other hand, a friend of mine recently bought a second-hand above-ground spa for $500 from a neighbor who was upgrading. He and some friends wheeled it home on a dolly and it cost him another $500 for wiring and set-up. I'm quite confident it added to the value of his property.

Thus, the economics of a spa are such that it will probably add value. But, it's probably not worth spending a lot of money on putting one in.

What's the Difference between In-Ground and Above-Ground?

An in-ground spa is essentially custom built. It's put in much the same way an in-ground swimming pool is installed. A hole is dug, it's lined with sand, and then, typically, a concrete (gunite) or fiberglass body is laid into it. Pipes and wiring are installed at the same time leading off to a separate location where a pump, filter, heater, blower, and power source for lights are located. The surrounding ground is cemented over, often bricked in as part of a patio and, within a few months, you have an in-ground spa. You can see why it's so expensive to build.

Yes, it's wonderful to use, adds enormously to the appearance of the backyard. But, except in very upscale homes, it's unlikely you'll add that much value to your home.

An above-ground spa, on the other hand, is quite different. All that's required is a power source, typically 220 volts, but 110 will sometimes be enough. And you need to choose a good location.

The above-ground spa itself normally is totally self-contained. It has the pumps, filter, heater, and all controls built around it. The sides, typically around three feet tall, are usually made of some type of stained wood that compliments the spa's fiberglass body. Installation usually means preparing a flat spot of ground, leveling it out with some sand, and carting the spa in.

Once it's connected to the power supply, you fill it with water from a hose and turn it on. (To maintain water purity, there are chemicals that must be used.) Both in-ground and most above-ground spas usually require a building permit for installation. As far as many buyers are concerned, this above-ground spa will add as much value as an in-ground spa.

How Big and What Color?

These are essentially questions of taste and, with a spa, it probably doesn't matter. Spas come in a wide variety of colors, often tan or dark blue. Since the color influences the salability of the spa, the manufacturers almost always pick the most popular colors, so it's unlikely you'll go wrong.

When it comes to size, keep in mind that although smaller is less expensive, you want a spa that can easily hold two people. Unfortunately, manufacturers sometimes exaggerate how many people can fit into their spa. My own rule is that if you get a spa that's rated to hold four, you're fairly safe that it can very comfortably hold two.

Maintenance Can Be Tough

Many owners decide to put in a spa for two reasons: (1) They are aware that it can help sell their house for more, but their real motivation is (2) to be able to it use themselves. If that's your situation, then you should be aware of the difficulties in maintaining a spa.

Because the spa is so small, at least when compared to a swimming pool (it's large when compared to a bathtub!), the assumption is that it's easy to maintain. Nothing could be further from the truth.

Consider a swimming pool that may have 20,000 gallons of water. At the least, you will want to maintain the ph (acid/base balance) so the water isn't harsh on the skin and you'll want to be sure the level of bacteria in the water is low so anyone using it doesn't get an infection. Typically, this means frequently testing the water, then balancing the pool using acid or base and adding chlorine to specified levels.

Now, a couple of people jump into the pool. They may displace 50 gallons of water and will contribute to increasing the bacterial count and changing the acid/base balance. However, 50 gallons out of 20,000 is, so to speak, a drop in the bucket. You can put 10 people in that pool and still not have a huge and immediate effect.

On the other hand, the spa is typically only 500 gallons. Displace 50 gallons and that's 10 percent of the total. Because the water is hot, the chlorine (or bromine which is often used as an oxidizing agent in spas) quickly disappears. Further, the ph balance is hard to maintain.

All of which is to say that with a spa, you will constantly be fighting to keep the water balanced and safe. Additionally, there will be problems of murky water (because most spa filters simply are too small to do the job they are called upon to do), and foaming, which happens when the same water is constantly churned and recirculated.

Simply flushing out the water and starting from scratch won't help, because the new water must be chemically balanced and oxidized. I have been a spa owner and know many others who have, too, and spending $50 or more a month on chemicals is not uncommon, nor is it unusual to be constantly dickering with it.

You can hire a spa service to come in and handle it all for you, at around $50 to $100 per month.

A spa is wonderful to own, to use, and if purchased and installed inexpensively, can be a plus when you sell. However, maintaining it is not a bed of roses.

$$

Fix a bad pool.

People often talk about putting in a pool as a way of adding value to a home, but almost never will you hear them speak of fixing or removing a troubled pool to increase value. Yet, fixing or getting rid of a bad pool is much more important than adding a new one.

As far as adding a new pool is concerned, today it's virtually priced itself out of consideration. Unless you own a million dollar home in the Southwest, I would never recommend putting in a swimming pool. The cost, which today can easily be $50,000 or more, is phenomenal. And, except for the high-priced homes I just mentioned, most buyers would like, but don't expect a swimming pool. (Indeed, many older buyers prefer a home without a pool!)

The rule here is easy: Just forget about the pool.

On the other hand, what if your home already has a pool put in years ago either by you or by a former owner? (In some areas of Los Angeles, virtually every home on the block in many neighborhoods has a pool!)

If the pool is good, then maintain it, and it will be a plus when you sell. But, if the pool is bad, deal with it. It's lowering the value of your property.

What Is a Bad Pool?

It's kind of like a backache. If you have it, you'll know it. I've owned many homes with pools and all except one (my current home) were bad in one way or another. Here are some of the typical problems that can cause a pool to be bad and require fixing:

- *Cracks:* Pools that were improperly built or which were built on ground that shifts can crack. When this happens, the pool is severely damaged. It's sort of like having a boat with a hole in it except here the water goes out instead of coming in. A fix typically requires draining the pool and having professionals patch the crack. It can be costly, but it should be done or the buyer will severely reduce the price offered for the house. In some cases, the damage is so severe the crack can't be fixed. In that case, see page 212.

- *Algae:* Algae grows in water whenever the bacteria count goes up, typically in the hot days of summer. There are at least three types of algae:

  —The first is colored green. You can sometimes see green algae floating or attached to the side of the pool. It is the easiest to remove and can usually be dealt with by just increasing the chlorine levels (or super-chlorinating the pool) and cleaning the filter.

  —The next is yellow, which will typically begin forming around nooks and crannies and inlets in the pool. It is more stubborn and must often be scraped off. Strong chemicals can also be used to reduce or eliminate it.

  —Black algae, however, is the worst because it has often eaten right into the plaster. If not removed by strong chemicals and scraping, the pool may need to be drained and acid-washed (that is, a weak acid solution is scrubbed on the plaster to remove the black algae). You cannot, however, acid-wash a pool more than a few times without permanently damaging the plaster.

  Unfortunately, if untreated, the progression is usually from green to yellow to black. Thus, if you have a pool, constant vigilance is the way to avoid costly problems.

- *Pump and filter problems:* Pumps go out and can cost hundreds of dollars to replace. Filters, if not changed regularly, can deteriorate and also cost hundreds of dollars to replace.

- *Bad piping:* Sometimes the pipes leading to the pool will corrode. This is typically the case for older pools where copper pipes were used. The acid used to balance the pool's ph (if used in excess) can dissolve the copper, sometimes very quickly. The cost of replacing bad piping, particularly if it is connected to the bottom drain of the pool, can be many thousands of dollars, if it can even be done at all.

- *Floating:* Although it may seem strange, pools themselves can float. If you drain a pool when the surrounding water table is high, you can literally float the pool out of the ground. I once had a home where the former owners began draining the pool right after the rainy season when the water table was high. The shallow end emptied first and with no water inside to hold it down, that end of the pool popped up several inches. Of course, they immediately re-filled it with water, but the damage was done. One end was several inches higher than the other. Fixing it would have required virtually rebuilding the pool. So, I put in new decking at a higher level and cosmetically landscaped around it until the eye was fooled by the problem, unless you looked closely. Of course, I disclosed the problem to prospective buyers and I turned a liability into an asset.

- *Electrical short:* This is a serious problem. Most pools have underwater lights. Unless the lights and electrical cables are sealed, they can get wet and can introduce electricity right into the water. There have been cases where people have died of electrical shock from bad wiring and lights. Every pool should be professionally tested for electricity in the water and either the lights or wiring professionally fixed or permanently disconnected.

What about the Hopeless Pool?

I have seen individuals with hopeless problems (cracks, floating, and so on) simply give up on their pools. In several cases, they filled them with dirt and sand and then planted a garden inside. Of course, this must be done correctly with holes knocked into the side of the pool, or else it's the same as putting a plant in a pot without a way for excess water to get out. Water will tend to gather at the bottom and cause rotting and mold.

In another case, an owner hired a crew with a bulldozer to come in and dig out the pool. It was quite a mess for a week or so. And it cost nearly $7,000 to do. But, in the end, the owner figured it added that much and more to the property *not* to have a bad pool.

The moral here is that if you have a good pool, maintain it. If you have a bad pool, fix it. And if you have an impossible pool, look for a creative solution.

TECHNIQUE **50**

Create a "Things To Do" organizer.

Which techniques are you going to use? Which ones can you simply ignore? Here's an organizer to help determine what makes sense for you . . . and what doesn't. Remember, not all techniques will give you a profit. All, however, are designed to make your home more saleable in today's highly competitive market . . . and to make it sell for more money.

[ ]   **Make a better first impression.**
       I need to work on this.   _____
       I'm okay here.   _____

[ ]   **Don't park in your driveway.**
       I need to work on this.   _____
       I'm okay here.   _____

[ ]   **Give your house a friendly look.**
       I need to work on this.   _____
       I'm okay here.   _____

[ ]   **Fix that lawn.**
       I need to work on this.   _____
       I'm okay here.   _____

[ ]   **Add new outside lighting.**
       I need to work on this.   _____
       I'm okay here.   _____

[ ]   **Clear out the debris.**
      I need to work on this.   _____
      I'm okay here.   _____

[ ]   **Dump the old couches.**
      I need to work on this.   _____
      I'm okay here.   _____

[ ]   **Replace your home's jewelry.**
      I need to work on this.   _____
      I'm okay here.   _____

[ ]   **Get rid of house odors.**
      I need to work on this.   _____
      I'm okay here.   _____

[ ]   **Hang pictures from the masters.**
      I need to work on this.   _____
      I'm okay here.   _____

[ ]   **Take neighborhood action.**
      I need to work on this.   _____
      I'm okay here.   _____

[ ]   **Push your HOA.**
      I need to work on this.   _____
      I'm okay here.   _____

[ ]   **Form a NAC.**
      I need to work on this.   _____
      I'm okay here.   _____

[ ]   **Get allied with a painter/paint.**
        I need to work on this.   _____
        I'm okay here.   _____

[ ]   **Go after graffiti.**
        I need to work on this.   _____
        I'm okay here.   _____

[ ]   **Go after blighters.**
        I need to work on this.   _____
        I'm okay here.   _____

[ ]   **Get city hall on your side.**
        I need to work on this.   _____
        I'm okay here.   _____

[ ]   **Work on the school.**
        I need to work on this.   _____
        I'm okay here.   _____

[ ]   **Contact public works.**
        I need to work on this.   _____
        I'm okay here.   _____

[ ]   **Go see the parks and recreation
        department.**
        I need to work on this.   _____
        I'm okay here.   _____

[ ]   **Redo your driveway.**
        I need to work on this.   _____
        I'm okay here.   _____

[ ]   **Mend your fences.**
        I need to work on this.   _____
        I'm okay here.   _____

[ ]   **Make over the front.**
        I need to work on this.   _____
        I'm okay here.   _____

[ ]   **Add a tile entrance.**
        I need to work on this.   _____
        I'm okay here.   _____

[ ]   **Hang a chandelier.**
        I need to work on this.   _____
        I'm okay here.   _____

[ ]   **Separate rooms.**
        I need to work on this.   _____
        I'm okay here.   _____

[ ]   **Improve the floors.**
        I need to work on this.   _____
        I'm okay here.   _____

[ ]   **Add décor.**
        I need to work on this.   _____
        I'm okay here.   _____

[ ]   **Add light.**
        I need to work on this.   _____
        I'm okay here.   _____

[ ]   **Remove popcorn ceilings.**

I need to work on this.   _____

I'm okay here.   _____

[ ]   **Paint lively.**

I need to work on this.   _____

I'm okay here.   _____

[ ]   **Frame your home in molding.**

I need to work on this.   _____

I'm okay here.   _____

[ ]   **Make your kitchen over.**

I need to work on this.   _____

I'm okay here.   _____

[ ]   **Put in a kitchen floor/countertop.**

I need to work on this.   _____

I'm okay here.   _____

[ ]   **Replace kitchen appliances.**

I need to work on this.   _____

I'm okay here.   _____

[ ]   **Do a bathroom restoration.**

I need to work on this.   _____

I'm okay here.   _____

[ ]   **Relight your home.**

I need to work on this.   _____

I'm okay here.   _____

[ ]   **Add a new bathroom.**
I need to work on this.   _____
I'm okay here.   _____

[ ]   **Convert an attic.**
I need to work on this.   _____
I'm okay here.   _____

[ ]   **Finish off a basement.**
I need to work on this.   _____
I'm okay here.   _____

[ ]   **Organize closets.**
I need to work on this.   _____
I'm okay here.   _____

[ ]   **Convert a room.**
I need to work on this.   _____
I'm okay here.   _____

[ ]   **Add an extra room.**
I need to work on this.   _____
I'm okay here.   _____

[ ]   **Replace single-pane windows.**
I need to work on this.   _____
I'm okay here.   _____

[ ]   **Replace interior doors.**
I need to work on this.   _____
I'm okay here.   _____

[ ]   **Landscape low.**
        I need to work on this.   _____
        I'm okay here.   _____

[ ]   **Landscape high.**
        I need to work on this.   _____
        I'm okay here.   _____

[ ]   **Add a spa.**
        I need to work on this.   _____
        I'm okay here.   _____

[ ]   **Fix a bad pool.**
        I need to work on this.   _____
        I'm okay here.   _____

Index

Bathroom(s) *(Continued)*
    painting, 140, 160
    shower, 159, 160
    sink/faucet, 159
    size, 158
    tiling, 158, 159
    towel racks, 160
    tub refinishing, 160
    whirlpool bath, 158, 159
Bedroom(s):
  addition, 188
  conversion, 181–184, 218
    cost cutting, 184
    creating one large master
      bedroom suite from two
      small, 182
    do-it-yourself, 184
    plumbing rerouting, 184
    removing walls, 182–183
    sheetrock, 184
  removing furniture/clutter, 5–6
  value of (number of, relative to
    total square footage),
    181–182
Blighters, going after, 70–74, 215
Blinds, wood, 44
Bushes/shrubbery, 11–13, 200–204.
  See also Landscaping

Car parking, 7–10
Carpeting:
  cleaning, 121
  importance of, 120–121
  removing discarded piles of, 25
  replacing, 120–123

Ceilings:
  basement, 175
  popcorn, 133–136, 217
Chandeliers, 112–115, 216
  avoiding gaudiness, 113
  cost, 112–113
  in dining room, 115
  in entrance hall, 112–115
  renting, 113–115
City hall (getting on your side),
  75–79, 215
  being alert, 75–76
  getting organized, 76
  getting public support, 76
  learning your rights, 76
  observing deadlines, 76
  planning a long fight,
    76–79
Cleanup, 23–26, 214
  carpet cleaning, 121
  clutter removal, 2–6
  common debris, 23–26
  drainage, 25–26
  driveway, 96
  homeowners' association
    demands for, 52
  interior walls (*vs.* repainting),
    137–138
Closets, 177–180, 218
  built-in organizers, 179–180
  cost, 179
  do-it-yourself, 180
  improvements to make,
    178–179
  smells, 178–179